THE NORTH COUNTRY MURDER *of* IRENE IZAK

I0805735

THE NORTH COUNTRY MURDER *of* IRENE IZAK

STAINED BY HER BLOOD

DAVE SHAMPINE

Foreword by RAYMOND O. POLETT, NEW YORK STATE POLICE (RETIRED)
Introduction by PAUL EWASKO & LISA CAPUTO

THE History PRESS

Published by The History Press
Charleston, SC 29403
www.historypress.net

Cover image courtesy of the Thousand Islands Bridge Authority and Helen Ewasko.

First published 2010
Second printing 2011
Third printing 2011

Manufactured in the United States

ISBN 978.1.60949.119.2

Library of Congress Cataloging-in-Publication Data

Shampine, Dave.
The North Country murder of Irene Izak : stained by her blood / Dave Shampine.
p. cm.
ISBN 978-1-60949-119-2
1. Izak, Irene Juliana, 1942-1968. 2. Murder victims--New York (State)--Biography. 3. Murder--Investigation--New York (State)--Case studies. I. Title.
HV6533.N5S53 2010
364.152'3092--dc22
2010041895

To the memory of

Lialia

Her fate was undeserved.
Her killer goes unpunished.
For him justice awaits in Eternity.
Her family can only pray.

CONTENTS

FOREWORD

I was asked by Dave Shampine to write this forward. My first reaction was to decline, but it is out of respect and friendship for Dave that I do so.

It seems like a short time ago that I was roused from sleep at two o'clock in the morning. A friend of mine, Sergeant DeGroot, told me that a female body had been found on Wellesley Island in the St. Lawrence River. I was awake instantly and asked DeGroot if he had called my partner, Charlie "Chip" Donoghue. He advised me that he had called Chip first.

I dressed, got in my police car and sped to the scene, arriving about 2:45 a.m. I was met by Donoghue and uniformed officers.

What followed over the next few years is a convoluted tale that completely took over my life for the rest of my career. When Captain George Dana (the recently promoted captain in charge of the Bureau of Criminal Investigation, or BCI) arrived at the scene, he introduced himself to me and promptly advised me that this was my case to run with. He also allotted a phalanx of BCI men to work with me. My job was to assign these men as needed, collect their findings and, in the first ten days, compile a full report to Division Headquarters in Albany.

Several factors made this case so difficult. The location of the murder was 1.1 miles from the Canadian border. At the time of day of the murder, all government offices were closed. The lousy weather obliterated evidence, the rain blotting out footprints and fingerprints. The lack of vehicular traffic afforded the killer quick egress from the scene. There were few tourists and year-round residents to hear or see anything. In normal weather, the island would have been bustling with tourists, fishermen and the like, allowing investigators to conduct meaningful interviews and perhaps gather supportive evidence.

Putting all of that aside, it was my case to solve, and I could not solve it. I take full responsibility, and I will think about this case for the rest of my days.

Raymond O. Polett, New York State Police (ret.)
Punta Gorda, Florida

ACKNOWLEDGEMENTS

Several years before the Irene Izak murder investigation came back to life in 1998, a state police investigator took me into his confidence, telling me his beliefs about who murdered Irene on Wellesley Island. His hope, never realized, was to at least make an attempt to close the case.

Nowhere in these pages does his name appear, at his insistence. But to him I credit the planting of the seed, giving me the inspiration to move on with a story that has haunted former members of the New York State Police, several of whom have echoed his words and encouragement to me.

This project would never have been accomplished had it not been for the information shared with me by Raymond O. Polett and his former investigative partner, the late Charles Donoghue, as well as private investigator Gus Papay. I salute their commitment.

Equally vital to this accomplishment was the assistance of Irene's sisters, Helen Ewasko and Luba Boyko; their brother, Zenon George; Helen's husband, Paul; and one of their daughters, Lisa Caputo. Their patience with my procrastinations, their endurance through my insistence for details and their understanding in the face of my mood swings and tantrums exemplify the beauty that lies within their hearts and souls.

To my team of copyeditors at the *Watertown Daily Times*—Mary Lu White, Patience O'Riley, Diana Staie and Cathie Egan—goes my thanks for reviewing my raw copy, making constructive suggestions and insisting that I learn the difference between "that" and "which." Mary Lu in particular has my appreciation for the interest, concern and moral support that she so kindly offered.

Transcribing voice recordings to paper, Zona Gale Sweeney simplified my task in bringing together the story that unravels in the pages that follow.

And finally, there was my wife, Lucille, who challenged my stubborn lack of confidence, insisting that I could get the job done. It took a while, but hopefully I rewarded her confidence in me.

INTRODUCTION

It wasn't meant to be.

Twenty-five-year-old Ukrainian-American Irene Izak loved anything and everything French. She was so fascinated by French culture and its language that in college she majored in French, went abroad to study in France and taught French to American high school students. When she suddenly learned of a teaching position in Montreal, Canada, nothing and no one could stop her from dropping everything and driving to Canada to apply for the job.

As she drove alone through upper New York State in the early morning hours of June 10, 1968, she was stopped by a state trooper, who claimed she was speeding in her Volkswagen Bug. After receiving a warning, she drove off for the city she hoped would become her new home. But it wasn't meant to be. A short distance later, she was found brutally murdered along the side of the road.

Irene's death had a profound effect on her entire family. It was as if a part of her father and mother had died with her, as they never were at peace, not knowing for certain who was responsible for killing her and why she was killed. So often the mere mention of Irene's ("Lialia's") name brought tears to her siblings' eyes; the pain was so deep that ultimately it was more comfortable not to mention her name. For years, each of the family members silently kept her in their memories, and rarely would anyone speak her name for fear that the grief would show itself through sobs and tears. The Izaks believed that there was no such thing as closure.

While Irene's nephews and nieces were under the age of twelve, they knew that something bad had happened to Aunt Lialia. One niece was so traumatized that she became preoccupied with her aunt's death and vowed that someday she would try to uncover more information about the murder, including the identification of the murderer. When she reached adulthood, she attempted to obtain written reports of her aunt's murder from the New York State authorities—to no avail. However, her determination drew her to the Internet, where she located a private investigator who instilled a good measure of discomfort in certain individuals who were unable to establish sufficient evidence connected to the perpetrator.

Soon thereafter, Dave Shampine took an even more active part in the investigation, as he had already been interested in Irene's slaying from his earliest days as a reporter. In loving tribute to Irene, this book honors her memory.

Yet the questions remain: What or who made her pull off the road? Was she tricked? Was she so rattled by the warning she received for allegedly speeding that she stopped to regain her composure and was then attacked? Who beat her so violently? Why did she have to die so young? Who did this to her?

Rest in peace, dear Irene. You live on in our hearts and have not been forgotten.

Paul Ewasko
Dalton, Pennsylvania

Lisa Caputo
Taylor, Pennsylvania

A BRIDGE SO CLOSE, SO FAR

The cold bit through us as we gathered at St. Vladimir's Cemetery on a hill overlooking the southern edge of Scranton, Pennsylvania. With a thirty-mile-per-hour wind swirling the previous night's snowfall about us in temperatures bottoming out at five degrees, we were wrapped in sadness, hope and, yes, even curiosity.

Sadness because, well, "nobody should be put through this," said my wife, Lucille, who was close to tears for a family she was just now meeting. Hope that a coffin might hold some shred of evidence that could finally bring a killer to justice. And curiosity: what might remain of a body interred three decades ago?

A contingent of New York State Police, along with a representative detail of their counterparts from Pennsylvania, had arrived on this morning of December 30, 1998, with heavy equipment to commence an exhumation. The state police investigators looked at me and a private detective, Augustine Papay, as if to ask, "What the hell are you doing here?" Indeed, that is exactly what they wanted to know, I would be told a couple weeks later.

Helen Ewasko had asked me to come. Helen, of nearby Dalton, Pennsylvania, and Luba Boyko of Conklin, New York, near Binghamton, were finally seeing the cops from New York State make a new effort to solve the long-unexplained murder of their sister, Irene Izak. While many murders go unsolved, this was a case in which the family felt they had been forgotten or perhaps ignored. As the none-too-shy Papay strongly suggested in his sharp-tongued Hungarian accent, maybe the state police did not want to solve it; maybe the case was an embarrassment to them. After all, a suspect in the investigation was one of their own: a state trooper.

As I joined Papay and the many family members who flanked Helen and Luba that morning at St. Vladimir's Cemetery, I admit I probably had a feeling of achievement, knowing that a two-part story that I had written for the *Watertown Daily Times* in northern New York contributed to bringing about this day's events. But I also feared that this might be an exercise in futility, one that would only bring more heartbreaking disappointments to a family who had had more than their share since that tragic day of June 10, 1968, when their "Lialia" Irene was bludgeoned to death on a New York island on the St. Lawrence River.

She was on her way to Canada. The attractive twenty-five-year-old, small-framed schoolteacher from Scranton was on the road after spending a week with relatives in Cleveland, Ohio.

A night or two before Irene began her final journey, she might have been warned in a dream of the fate that awaited. Screams in the middle of the night awakened Myron and Stefania Kowalsky in their Cleveland home. They rushed into the guest room and found their niece holding her head, weeping about her too realistic nightmare.

"Somebody was hitting me on the head," Irene cried.

When Irene set out in her Volkswagen on the afternoon of June 9, 1968, she was looking forward to a job interview in the province of Quebec, where she could use the French language that she had learned to love. But there was more on her mind than that.

"I want my freedom back, my old way of living," she wrote in a letter only two days before her fateful encounter.

The French language was not her only draw to Quebec. This was where she had suffered heartbreak from a severed relationship. Was she hoping to win him back?

In her childhood, Irene had been a refugee from the tyranny that embraced her Ukrainian homeland behind what became known as the Iron Curtain. Her upbringing was in a strictly religious home. Her father was a Catholic priest, one who could be married since he was of the Byzantine Rite.

Irene was anything but a rebellious student in an era of protest and violence, particularly on college campuses. Her entry into adult life was at a small Catholic college for women in Scranton. At Marywood College, where some one thousand young women were under the guidance of the Sisters of the Immaculate Heart of Mary, she was somewhat sheltered from the goings-on that rocked many campuses. Her demeanor was as might be expected of a young woman attending to her future at a religious institution.

Irene made her teaching debut in Binghamton, New York. Next came a teaching position in Rochester, New York. But that was behind her as she saw her future across a bridge, and the bridge was within sight at the very moment she was robbed of that future.

Along the road, she met New York state trooper David N. Hennigan. He was on patrol in a dark blue "concealed identity" car, scrutinizing Interstate 81 traffic in New York's Jefferson County for motorists who dared exceed the sixty-five-mile-per-hour speed limit.

David Hennigan was born in Watertown, the only child of a crushed stone company foreman. He attended Watertown High School, where he involved himself in few extracurricular activities. During his high school years, he worked as an orderly in Watertown's House of the Good Samaritan Hospital. When he graduated in 1957, the school's yearbook staff said of him, "He makes you laugh just like a clown; when he's around, you'll never frown."

Following graduation, he entered the army, which assigned him to Camp Leroy Johnson in Louisiana. He learned the skills of a medic, but his final tour of duty was as a military police officer at Camp Drum, on the outskirts of his hometown. From there, he stepped into the civilian police world, joining the New York State Police.

When he made his debut as a state trooper in 1962, a wire service photo appeared in his hometown paper, the *Watertown Daily Times*, showing him shaking hands with New York governor Nelson A. Rockefeller.

Trooper Hennigan was only a few days away from his sixth anniversary as a traffic cop when he came upon a woman driving alone in a tan 1965 Volkswagen, heading north on Interstate 81. Pulling the car over north of Watertown, the twenty-nine-year-old brown-eyed cop, married and the father of three, notified his desk sergeant, Gerald A. DeGroot, at 1:50 a.m. on Monday, June 10, that he was making a speed stop.

Nervously, Irene looked up at the six-foot-tall man in gray uniform, his Stetson hiding a thick crop of dark black hair and shadowing a ruggedly handsome face.

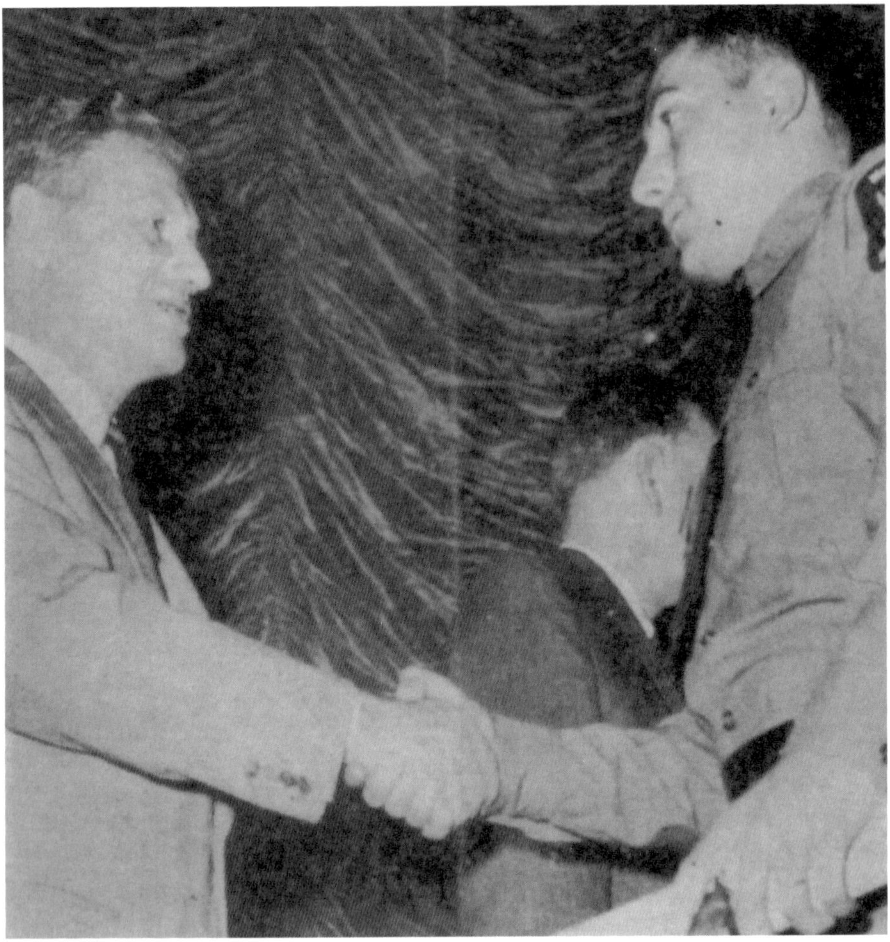

Governor Nelson Rockefeller congratulated new state trooper David Hennigan. *Associated Press Wire Photo, courtesy* Watertown Daily Times.

State police files are confidential because of the ongoing investigation, but later that year Jay Ettman, writing for *True Detective* magazine, suggested the conversation that transpired in that morning's darkness.

"You were exceeding the speed limit, Miss."

As Irene dug for a hand-sized plastic folder in her purse, the trooper said, "Just the license and registration."

"Was I really going fast?" she might have said.

As he compared the driver's appearance to the description on her license—blue eyes, five feet tall and 103 pounds—he asked her address.

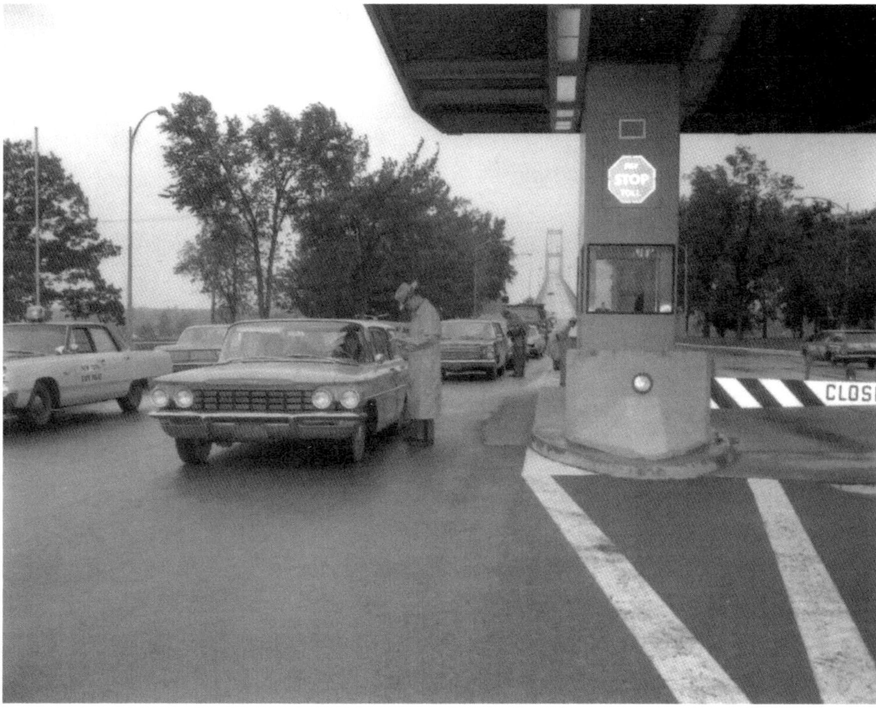

The tollbooth where Irene Izak talked nervously with an attendant before crossing the American span to Wellesley Island was closed to northbound traffic while state troopers questioned motorists leaving the island. *Courtesy* Watertown Daily Times.

When she said Scranton, he noted the New York tags on her car and a Rochester listing on her documents.

"I taught school in Rochester," she said.

He asked her destination.

"I'm on my way to Laval University in Quebec City."

Handing back her documents, the trooper dismissed her.

"I won't give you a citation this time," the Ettman article suggested Trooper Hennigan said. "Just a warning. Drive at the posted rate of speed, Miss. No faster."

The woman and the trooper both pulled away and continued north, never that far apart, with both proceeding all the way to the Thousand Islands Bridge, the first of three spans leading to Canada. Several minutes later, Irene reached the tollbooth for the bridge. At the far reach of the arched span lay Wellesley Island, destined to be Irene's final stop.

As Trooper Hennigan's car proceeded up the bridge at 2:09 a.m., Irene paid her one-dollar toll, talked briefly to the collector and then continued on her route. At the north end of the island, she anticipated reaching a second small bridge, which would take her across the international border onto Hill Island in the Canadian province of Ontario.

Trooper Hennigan, according to police, reported that he made rounds on Wellesley Island, doing property checks. He then backtracked before proceeding along the two-lane island road, called the Route 81 extension, that led traffic to the second span. The trooper came upon a wide pull-off, or rest area, that was just past the entrance to DeWolf Point State Park, a popular campground providing direct access to the river for fishermen and swimmers.

The Volkswagen that Trooper Hennigan had stopped on the mainland about forty-five minutes earlier, about twenty miles down the road, was now parked in the rest area. He reported that he found the car unoccupied.

Grabbing his flashlight, he inspected the car and its surroundings. Trooper Hennigan later told investigators that he spotted Irene's tinted anti-glare glasses in the gravel, just below the rear bumper of the Volkswagen. He called out her name and got no answer. The officer climbed down into a ten-foot-deep, shrubby and rock-studded ravine and searched "for several minutes," according to the Ettman account.

And then he found her. At 2:35 a.m., twenty-six minutes after he had passed the bridge tollbooth, Trooper Hennigan was on his car radio, notifying Sergeant DeGroot that he had discovered a homicide.

Police told the *Watertown Daily Times* that Irene's body was found facedown in a pool of blood. Fresh blood matted her light brown, shoulder-length hair. Her skull had been bludgeoned with several rocks with such force that her face had been driven two or three inches into the dirt.

The victim, clad in a dark pink sweater, beige slacks and leather sandals, had not been raped or sexually assaulted, the Jefferson County medical examiner in Watertown, Dr. Richard S. Lee, determined.

Death had occurred in a matter of a few minutes, the doctor said. "Multiple trauma to the cranium," caused by "blunt weapons—rocks," had resulted in "severe brain injury and hemorrhage," he noted in his autopsy report.

Police said the woman had not been robbed. Her purse appeared undisturbed in her car and still contained fifty-one dollars in cash and travelers' checks, as well as a credit card. Her class ring from Marywood College remained on her hand, and her watch was still on her wrist.

The keys to her car were on the ground near her body.

Meanwhile, as a fine drizzle and temperatures in the mid-fifties readied the approach of dawn, Trooper Hennigan explained to his colleagues that when he found the woman, he raised her head, trying to find traces of life. In doing that, he claimed he had stained his uniform with her blood.

State police in Jefferson County are members of a troop headquartered nearly one hundred miles away in Oneida, near Utica, New York. A few days after giving his account at the murder scene, Trooper Hennigan was summoned to Oneida to provide a more thorough statement of his encounters with Irene that night. The interview was never completed, at least not to the satisfaction of one of the investigators, Raymond O. Polett. The trooper's wife of nearly ten years, Beverly A. Sherlock Hennigan, rushed into an interrogation room and marched her husband away, according to Polett.

The trooper submitted to two polygraph tests, police say. The first was inconclusive, but he passed the second, according to Polett.

Months passed, turning into years, and the murder of Irene Izak remained unsolved. The investigation, by all appearances, sank deeply into dormancy.

More than two decades later, a woman in Taylor, Pennsylvania, who retained childhood memories of her Aunt Irene, started asking questions. Lisa Ewasko Caputo wanted to know what state police were doing, if anything, to bring this case to closure. The official responses gave her no satisfaction.

And then I stepped into the picture, unaware of Mrs. Caputo's search for the truth. The Izak case had shadowed my twenty-seven years of crime reporting in Jefferson County, and finally some state police members, both retirees and active personnel, were being more open with me about their suspicions. Investigators who now had the case file in their hands said they needed to talk to the one man known to have last seen Irene alive. But they doubted they would have the opportunity.

David Hennigan, now retired from the police world, had become a deacon in the Roman Catholic Church. He had taken the move to his second career while he was still a trooper, twelve years after his unforgettable experience on Wellesley Island.

Both intrigued and inspired by the candid comments from the veteran police officers, I interviewed by telephone Helen Ewasko; her brother, Zenon George Izak, of Warminster, Pennsylvania; and Ray Polett, who had retired to a beautiful waterfront property near Auburn, Pennsylvania.

And I tried to interview Deacon Hennigan, also by telephone. That was a mistake, since I could have tried visiting him. In my two attempts, I received no comments and a hang-up.

My two-part series about the murder of Irene Izak, based heavily on Polett's recollections and his first-time publicly expressed sentiments, appeared on June 10 and June 11, 1998, in the *Watertown Daily Times*.

Within a few days, Lisa Caputo introduced herself to me in a telephone call. Her family was retaining a private detective to seek answers, she said, and she asked for my assistance. My hope that my humble journalistic effort might spark movement in this old case was being fulfilled.

Little more than a month after my Izak series ran, I was meeting Gus Papay and his wife, Elizabeth, at a McDonald's restaurant in Watertown. I took him to the murder scene, and from there we teamed up in an effort to learn more about the investigation. Papay's goal was to motivate state police into reviving their investigation. And a motivator Papay was. Unafraid to step on toes, this retired New York City cop pushed Lisa's family, me and ultimately the governor of New York, George E. Pataki, to action.

A lengthy letter, signed by survivors of Irene Izak but actually written by Papay, urged Governor Pataki to reopen the investigation. The letter was passed on to state police superintendent James W. McMahon, and the effort that Lisa Caputo and I had separately hoped for was now a realization.

Finally, here we were on a wind-chilled cemetery hill, witnessing the first stage of what was to become an eight-month roller coaster ride of anticipations and letdowns. State police, reaching out to advances in police science, would never confirm that their focus was David Hennigan. But that became obvious to the church deacon on a June or July day in 1999, when state police pulled his car over on Interstate 81 near Watertown, inviting him to join them at a neutral location, a motel room, for a discussion.

He remained aloof to their investigation, refusing to talk to them, just as he had declined my request for an interview a year earlier.

His only public comment came when a New York City television reporter, Mary Murphy, did what I should have done, paying a surprise front door visit to his home near Dexter, New York, off shore of Lake Ontario.

"I had nothing to do with her death," Hennigan said in a filmed report that aired on August 19, 1999, on WB11 TV of New York and New Jersey.

But Irene Izak's blood, which had stained the trooper's uniform on a damp June morning in 1968, continued to stain the deacon's reputation more than three decades later.

IN SEARCH OF FREEDOM

A land in chaos greeted the newborn Irene Juliana Izak. She gasped her first breath and cried her first tears on July 22, 1942, in the Ukrainian village of Bolotnia, in the county of Peremyshl, a picturesque small community "surrounded by mountains on three sides as if they wanted to guard it against an enemy attack which was creeping from the east," as her father, Reverend Bohdan Izak, described in a letter.

Father Izak was thirty-four when, in April 1942, he arrived in Bolotnia to assume responsibility of his new Byzantine Catholic parish. He brought with him his pregnant wife, Maria Kowalsky Izak, two sons and two daughters. The firstborn, Andreey Ivan, was approaching his tenth birthday. Zenon Yuri was eight, Lubow Sophia Anna was about to turn seven and the youngest was four-year-old Olena Lydia.

It was not uncommon for a priest of the Byzantine Rite to be married if he took a wife before being ordained. Bohdan had been married five months prior to his 1932 ordination.

This was a family reunited. In 1939, Father Izak had been forced to tear his wife and children away from another village, Dobropole, where he was the parish priest, in order to escape religious persecution by the atheistic Bolshevik regime that ruled the land. Although she was only four at the time, his daughter Lubow, later anglicized to Luba, never forgot that dreary Sunday afternoon when she heard screams and cries:

> *I ran to the window and I saw people being forced onto wagons. I knew more or less what was going on, but I asked my mother anyway. She drew me away from the window, and she said not to watch. But these people, these Ukrainians, were being arrested and being taken to cattle cars and were being sent to Siberia.*

Her father was threatened; he was ordered to give up his faith and lead his people to socialism, she said. In the darkness of night, the priest whisked his family away, taking them to another village, Chesnyky, to be with his parents, John and Anna Izak. Then he left them behind, going into exile with other priests and seminarians in the Carpathian Mountains. He spent the next two years teaching, away from his loved ones.

Maria kept three of her children together under John Izak's roof, but Andreey was sent to another town where he could go to school. He stayed with his uncle Demetrius, who had a son about Andreey's age.

Two years later, on a day late in 1941, Luba was standing in the doorway of her grandmother's house when she saw a man dressed in black, wearing glasses, pass through the front gate. In her mind, doctors wore black and glasses.

"Grandmother, there's a doctor coming," she announced.

Olena, affectionately called Halya, was playing outside at the time. Afraid of the stranger, she ran into the house. Anna Izak immediately recognized the visitor to be her son, Bohdan.

Luba, embarrassed at not having known her father, ran and hid.

Father Izak had felt it safe to return, confident that invaders from Germany would free his homeland from religious tyranny. The arrival of Germany's Nazi war machine in 1941 was a welcomed sight in the Ukraine. In addition to religious suppression, the rule of the Bolsheviks had brought forced collectivization of agriculture and expropriation of produce. Famine struck, making life all the more difficult.

The invading army, nationalists hoped, would provide protection and the establishment of an independent Ukraine. The Germans were welcomed with open arms. Maria and her daughter Luba stood at the roadside with other townsfolk, waving wild poppies and cornflowers.

A repatriated Father Izak asked his bishop for a new parish, and he was awarded Bolotnia. And soon came the birth of his third daughter, who was named for an aunt, Irene, and an uncle, Julian. Her uncle Julian was at the time a soldier in a Ukrainian division, to become a German ally. But later, he would defect to fight with the Ukrainian underground and would be killed in an ambush by German soldiers.

"Irene was very special to my parents," said her sister Helen (Olena) Ewasko, "because my father had thought he would never see us again and my mother feared that something would happen to us."

As Father Izak had expected, he was free to publicly celebrate his faith under Nazi occupation. The fear that controlled the people under the Bolsheviks was gone, but the Germans were not benevolent conquerors, either. The Ukraine was having its usual harsh winter, and to feed themselves, the soldiers had no qualms about taking whatever food and livestock they wanted from the local folk.

On a day when the Nazis came to seize food, Father Izak pleaded for their mercy, pointing to his children. His mother-in-law, Sophia Kowalsky, was visiting, and she showed the soldiers a picture of her soldier son Julian. The German officer was unimpressed. After all, he had an army to feed.

The Izak family had little left to eat—only what Father Izak had the foresight to hide, as well as the scraps that his parishioners managed to gather for them. On this land provided by the parish, Father Izak raised grain, fruits and vegetables, some of which was preserved for the winter. Two cows, a pig, chickens, turkeys, geese and ducks provided the family's other needs.

And they had two horses, except that the Germans came and traded their tired nags for the Izaks' healthy mounts.

Bohdan and Maria Izak had a greater reason than hunger to fear the Germans, as Zenon discovered one day in their barn. While giving food and water to some pet rabbits, he felt a trickle of water drop from the loft above. And then he saw movement in the straw.

"Who's there," he screamed. There was no answer.

Terrified, he ran to his mother. She shared a secret: they were harboring some Jewish people in the barn and were bringing them food at night.

"If the Germans find out, we will all be killed," Maria warned her son.

Father Izak was also baptizing Jews to protect them from persecution. If he was found out, a horrible fate surely awaited the priest and his family.

Not all of the Germans were feared. One homesick soldier befriended the Izak family and was particularly taken by Luba, since he had a daughter about her age. Often he placed her on his knee and talked to her, although she understood little of his German tongue.

When the German occupation collapsed in the spring of 1944, the local people were again in despair. Father Izak described the situation in a letter written two years later to his sisters in Belgium and the United States:

> *German tanks and cars were moving east and west…Hordes of Ukrainian refugees are making their way to the west. Sadness, dejection and terror are reflected in their faces. We are all aware that the German front is crumbling and that sooner or later, the Bolsheviks will come.*

Receiving word that his mother was ill and was asking for him, Father Izak set out for Chesnyky on an April Sunday morning in his buggy, taking Andreey with him. As the day progressed, the townsfolk watched the Germans pull out.

During their stay in the village, the Nazis had taken over the schoolhouse to use as their headquarters. Now that the soldiers were departing, some children, including Luba, Zenon and Olena, went into the building to see what was left behind. Benches and pews had been pushed aside, and straw, which had served soldiers in their slumber, cluttered the floor.

Suddenly, a roar of planes shattered the peace of the sunny afternoon. Bombs fell on the village, one landing across the street from the school building and another right next to it. The schoolhouse shook, and the frightened, screaming children scrambled to the street and ran home. Racing behind them were flames jumping in a strong breeze from one thatched-roof house to another. Rapidly, the village became an inferno.

Fortunately for the Izak family, there were no houses between the school and their church, so their tin-roofed house, though not immune from the flying sparks, was spared. Maria grabbed her baby Irene from a crib and brought her down to the cellar, for fear that bombs might fall here, too.

The few German soldiers who had remained behind worked with other villagers to secure the parish house, tearing away any wood that was starting to burn. They also rescued livestock from four barns on the property.

Father Izak and his son returned that evening. After cresting a hill and seeing their beloved village in ruins, they rushed to find their family. Parishioners reassured them that Maria and the children were safe, and soon Father Izak was grasping his loved ones in his arms.

Three bombs had fallen less than two meters from the school, the priest learned. "Two meters to the right, our children would have perished under the ruins or would have been blown up by the bombs. Thus, the Blessed Virgin saved our children and our household goods," he said.

In the days that followed, a single Bolshevik plane continued daily bombing runs over or near Bolotnia. There were still Germans in hiding along the river Hnyla Lypa, west of Bolotnia, and they used Ukrainian laborers to dig barricades for their lines of defense. Father Izak, preparing his family for yet another trial as refugees, went to the Germans with a trade offer. He had two piglets, and he needed two strong horses to pull his wagon. The army may have needed its horses, but the soldiers needed food, too. The trade was accomplished, although as time passed, it would prove to be meaningless for the family. The Izaks' flight was still two months away.

Father Izak contacted his brother-in-law, Josaphat Kowalsky, who lived about 155 miles to the west, to arrange routes and means of travel. Again with the help of his parishioners, he stocked food and clothing supplies. Early in July 1944, they were ready to depart.

"We were fretting," the priest wrote. "We bid farewell to Maria's mother, who with a heart in turmoil, arrived early Monday morning. Early in the evening, Mother sat in the wagon, and everyone started to cry. Would we see each other again in this lifetime?"

At the railroad station a day later, Father Izak arranged to place his family on a boxcar on a freight train. They loaded the supplies they had mustered, as well as a cow and the crib because baby Irene couldn't sleep without it. The cow was at one end of the car, with hay and straw, while the family was settled at the opposite end.

Their journey was beginning "in the last hour," Father Izak wrote, just as the German defenses were collapsing. Sadness and fear weighed heavily on the family, not only in anticipation of the unknown but also of what might be their immediate fate.

One night, as the train steamed along its westbound route, Andreey and Zenon overheard a conversation in a nearby compartment: "We will slaughter the Ukrainians." They told their father, who locked the doors of the boxcar. After the train stopped at Chiriv, somebody detached the Izaks' coach, the last on the train. The strangers wanted to leave behind the boxcar so that they could later in the night rob and murder the family, Father Izak believed.

With the train about to pull away, Father Izak ran to the stationmaster pleading for help. The stationmaster was also Ukrainian, so he delayed the train to hitch the last coach.

This first leg of their journey to freedom lasted three days and three nights. "Lialia Irene slept well at night because the train rocked her," her father wrote.

Being the youngest child, Irene was "so much pampered," her brother Zenon recalled. "She was very pretty, and looking like a doll with her curly hair, so someone in the family named Irene Lialia, meaning doll, and it stuck," he said.

Father Izak milked the cow to provide nourishment for his children during the trip. After reaching the Kowalsky home at Liska, Father Izak set out alone for a return to Bolotnia. He had planned to return for more belongings, which he would haul on a cart using those horses he had bartered from the Germans. But he found backtracking not as simple as the westward train ride. His train stopped at Pidzamko, about fifty-two miles away from Bolotnia, and could proceed no farther because of the Bolshevik takeover.

The determined priest, having exhausted his food and drink supplies, continued his journey on foot, except for a four-mile breather when he hitched a ride on a German tank. Fatigue and deprivation diluted his eagerness, especially as he encountered a massive flow of westbound refugee traffic, civilians and Nazis alike. His legs were numb, and to hunger he attributed the black spots that he saw dancing in his eyes. His mission was surrendering to despair.

"You won't get there today," he thought. "And what will be if tomorrow my legs won't serve me, if the Bolsheviks cut you off. You'll get to Bolotnia, and what will you do if the Germans took your horses, or the Partisans? How will you get to Maria and the children?"

He remembered the fear that he saw in Maria when he left her at Liska "Maria, my Maria!" he cried. "Children, my children!"

A German ambulance in the midst of the refugee flow stopped near him. There was no room in the vehicle for another passenger, but the priest, abandoning his mission, was permitted to ride on a fender, en route to another reunion with his family.

On July 16, 1944, back in the arms of his wife, "we thank the Blessed Virgin for her help in rescuing me," he wrote.

After a week in Liska, it was time to begin their long journey to freedom. While rumors about executions back home left them in mourning, they monitored the continuing advance of the Bolsheviks. The escape would not be easy. Partisan groups were roaming in the Carpathian forest and had damaged railroad tracks.

For two liters of whiskey and two liters of honey, two German soldiers drove the Izak and Kowalsky families, four adults and six children, in a pickup truck about twelve miles to a border town, Kamanchi. There, they hid for five days, until arrangements for train transportation were made.

A cargo train of forty-five lorries—wagons without walls or roofs—awaited. "On such a lorry, we were loaded, twenty-one of us," Father Izak wrote. The refugees made a roof of sheets and blankets, which, they later found, was inadequate protection from rainfall. As crowded as they were on this lorry, only women and children could sprawl out for sleep. The men sat up.

They pulled out of Kamanchi on July 30 and the next day passed another border town, Lupkiv, there crossing into Slovakia.

"Each one of us, with our thoughts and hearts, kiss the last boundary of his motherland and his family, which was left behind to a horrible fate," the priest wrote.

The train ride lasted nine days and nine nights, passing through Hungary before reaching Vienna, Austria. During the stops along the way, the priest crawled in fields looking for vegetation suitable to feed his family.

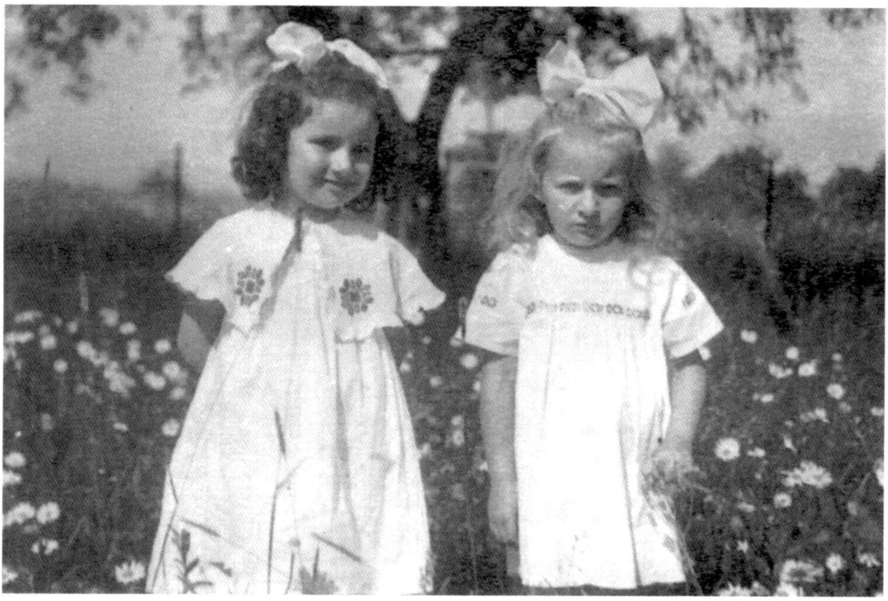

Cousins Irene and Nusia. *Courtesy Helen Ewasko.*

"At the main stations of Hungary, we displayed our baby Irene, and my brother-in-law's Nusia. Irene, curly and dark-haired, and Nusia, blonde and curly-haired, like two live dolls, captivated the Hungarian women. As a result, the children were brought bread, beets and other foods."

Leaving the train at Vienna, the refugees were led to a large, crowded "transitional camp" at Strasshof. The sight of this place, with its wire fences, and the stories that had circulated about persecution of the Jews were frightening to the child Luba:

> *The women were separated from the men. Mother, carrying Irene, took us girls and dad took the boys, and we were taken into this building and told to take off our clothes. I'm terribly terribly embarrassed for mother. They take us into the next room and I look up in the ceiling and there are these things that I see, and I thought we were going to be gassed. I thought we were in the gas chamber.*

Actually, it was a delousing station. They were showered, aware that German soldiers were watching, laughing and making fun of them. Then they were led to a bunkhouse to stay the night.

"Dad and Mom stayed up all night killing the bugs because, the irony is, after they put us through all this delousing thing and we were clean, they put us into these straw bunks which were full of lice," Luba said.

For the ten days that followed in this camp, Father Izak rigged up an outdoor shelter with blankets. Coffee and a slice of bread were served them for breakfast and supper, while beet soup sufficed for lunch. If they were to remain at this camp, Father Izak heard, the Germans would likely move them to a labor station. He and Josaphat Kowalsky established contact with a woman working in the camp. In exchange for two gold rings belonging to Josaphat's wife, Alexandra, including her wedding band, the German woman provided papers and a driver to help them slip away.

They were secreted off to a farm not far from the camp and were allowed the shelter of an attic above a chicken coop. For three weeks, they endured this hideaway. Father Izak, meanwhile, searched nearby villages for a place to settle his family. He expected support from his counterparts of the Roman Rite, but "they spoke with me on the stoop of their palace." None of these Austrian priests offered a place for them to stay.

Finally, on September 17, 1944, Father Izak found a modest house, with one room and a kitchen for the seven Izaks and three Kowalskys, in Bockfliess, three miles from Strasshof. The locals were astonished to see a married Catholic priest. He was allowed to celebrate his Mass at a side altar in the Roman Catholic church, but he found the parish priest otherwise unaccommodating.

"He told me to buy my own communion wine for Mass, although there were large vineyards in Bockfliess and there was plenty of wine available," Father Izak wrote.

As more refugees poured into the area that winter, many were taken into the Izak-Kowalsky home while they looked for a more permanent shelter. Among these were other Byzantine priests with their families, including the priest who had united Bohdan and Maria in marriage.

As spring arrived in 1945, time had come for the refugees to take flight again. The Bolsheviks were crossing international borders and were moving fast. The two families decided they should follow separate paths of escape. Bidding farewell to the Kowalskys, with promises to meet again under a flag of freedom, the Izaks obtained a ride on a truck. Their next stop, on March 12, was Vienna.

The Austrian city was being showered by American bombs, and the train station was a pile of burning rubble. Fortunately, one set of tracks was still intact. A train was leaving in two hours, but it was already packed. Father Izak saw that there seemed to be no room for a family of seven:

> *I felt a tremendous surge of energy and took in my arms each child and with a firm plea, passed them through each window into the hands of the passenger who happens to be there. The children are scattered throughout the entire wagon. Then, I quickly pleaded with a German officer who observed the entire episode.*

The soldier helped Father Izak lift the small-framed Maria and pushed her through the window into the car. Father Izak managed to position himself on a step of the car and held his place there as the train pulled away from the Vienna station. Later, as some passengers left the train at subsequent stops, the family was able to regroup and assess what belongings they had managed to salvage during the frantic train boarding. They got off at a village about sixty miles from Vienna, but the stay was brief. With word that Vienna had fallen to the Bolsheviks, the flight had to continue. Father Izak now faced more despair, but this time it was not his: "Maria was exhausted and became resigned to her fate. She is ready to die and doesn't want to run anymore."

He pleaded with her, explaining there was no sense in giving up after having come so far. "We have to save our children," he urged.

They knew they had to go north, since it appeared likely that Americans, not Bolsheviks, would be taking possession of that region. And once again, it was a German soldier who came to the rescue, driving the family to the city of Linz.

"Mother of God, you continue to save us," Father Izak prayed.

At Linz, the children were taken into a convent, where the nuns bathed and fed them. Then, the family boarded a train that took them to Taufkirchen, on the river Pram. There, on April 12, 1945, Father Izak marched his raggedly dressed family to a parish house and presented a letter of introduction from the bishop at Linz. The priest dutifully took them into his home.

About three weeks later, on May 12, freedom appeared at hand for the refugees: American soldiers victoriously marched into the village.

But more struggles, though dwarfed by their past experiences, soon would test the family. A new assistant parish priest was assigned to the village, so the pastor evicted his refugee guests. First they were given a rotting house within sight and smell of the village outhouse. Father Izak again found himself pleading to a fellow priest for dignified shelter. It won his family an attic room in the parish's horse barn.

Late in August, Maria and one of the children, Zenon, became ill. After a week, a doctor determined that it was typhoid, and an American drove them to a hospital at Scherding. Father Izak was left to take care of their other four children in a barn bearing a sign: "Typhoid—entrance forbidden." The hospitalization lasted a few days, until tests proved their illness had been misdiagnosed. Even so, the community wanted nothing to do with any of the Ukrainian refugees. Villagers and their American occupiers told the Ukrainians to go back to their homeland.

Father Izak rode a bicycle to Scherding to protest and was arrested by an American army lieutenant. Maria, still ill, also went to Scherding to seek support and found a sympathetic major. The major informed his subordinate that there would be no forced repatriation.

The Izaks remained in Taufkirchen into 1946, when they began receiving care packages from the American Red Cross. But Father Izak, now rejoined by Josaphat and Alexandra Kowalsky with their daughter Nusia, knew that he was not welcome in this village.

"The local community, the parish priest and the parishioners, do not look kindly at us," he wrote late that year as he concluded his diary. "They only tolerate us because they must. We have already grown accustomed to this and have learned to bear it."

There was hope, however. Father Izak had an older sister who, as a teenager many years earlier, had immigrated to the United States. Xenia Haas of Canandaigua, New York, and another sister in Belgium, Zosia Izak, arranged to sponsor his family for emigration across the ocean. Freedom, as they had never before enjoyed it, awaited them.

SAFE IN AMERICA

"We are going to be safe," Luba Izak thought as she saw New York Harbor in the distance. "We are going to be safe now."

This was an emotion that the twelve-year-old had never felt before. Her father, the Reverend Bohdan Izak, was observing his fortieth birthday by leading his family of seven to the Promised Land, the United States of America. As the USS *Marine Jumper*, a military transport ship, sailed within sight of the big city on the evening of April 18, 1948, its excited refugee passengers watched in awe.

"The lights were so beautiful," Luba said. "We were close enough to the shore that you could see the city lights, and the streetlights were strung like necklaces. Just beautiful!"

The ocean crossing of about ten days had not been easy, particularly for Maria Izak, forty, and her daughters Luba and Olena (who was now ten). Much of the time—while assigned to the B deck, separated from the males of the family, who were quartered on a lower deck—the three were seasick. Actually, the gentlemen found themselves not so seaworthy either.

But the youngest, Irene, about to turn six in three months, was making the most of this adventure. She found many ways to make sport on the cruise, and when her older sisters were feeling better, she drafted them into games of hide-and-seek.

The arrival at New York Harbor was trying for an anxious family. All of the refugees were delayed on their ship for another day while immigration officers checked the legitimacy of their documents. They were then taken to a railroad station, their next stop being Philadelphia.

A distant cousin, another Ukrainian priest, was expected to meet the Izaks at the train, but he never arrived. Instead, they were greeted in Philadelphia by two strangers, members of the cousin's parish. On their ride to the priest's rectory in Bridgeport, Pennsylvania, the Izaks were taking their first looks at an American way of life.

"As we were traveling along the city streets, we marveled," said Luba.

> *We couldn't believe! Because we were looking at fruit and vegetables that were out in the open. Everything was open. We couldn't believe the food because all those years that we were escaping, and even in Austria, we were always hungry and never was there enough food. We didn't know that people could eat so well.*

Before leaving Europe, Father Izak had written to Archbishop-Metropolitan Constantine Bohachevsky in Philadelphia, asking for help in relocating in the United States. The prelate lent the priest money to pay the family's boat fare and prepared a mission for him—the formation of a Byzantine Rite Catholic parish at Colchester, Connecticut. Polish and Ukrainian immigration to the United States had begun before World War I, and many of the immigrants had filtered into Connecticut, where most went to work on farms. While the Polish were familiar with the Roman Catholic Church, the people from the Ukraine needed spiritual guidance similar to what they were accustomed to in their homeland. They turned to the Greek Orthodox faith, which was not in union with the Church of Rome. Father Izak's task was to bring them back to Catholicism.

Late in April, the family was occupying the second floor of a house in Colchester, the ground floor of which was turned into a chapel. Here was founded the Dormition of the Holy Mother of God Ukrainian Catholic Church, later shortened to St. Mary's Ukrainian Catholic Church.

Three of the children—Andreey, fifteen, becoming Andrew; Zenon, fourteen; and Luba—were soon walking three blocks to school, with pleas from their parents that they set an example.

"We must never do anything that would bring shame on my parents," Luba said. "I just grew up with that, that I must always do the right thing and I must always be kind. I must always look out for other people."

They spoke only a smattering of English, words that an old woman had taught them in Austria. But the children, picking up their new language

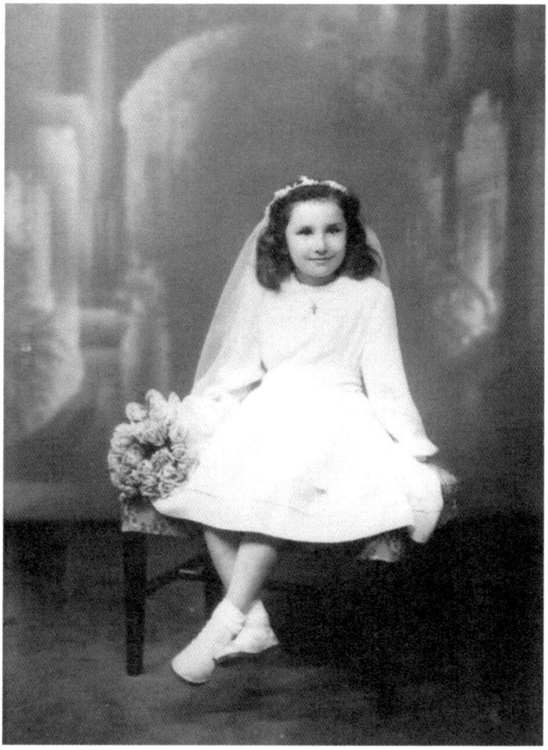

Right: Irene on First Communion day. *Courtesy Helen Ewasko.*

Below: Irene with her siblings and cousin Nusia. *Courtesy Helen Ewasko.*

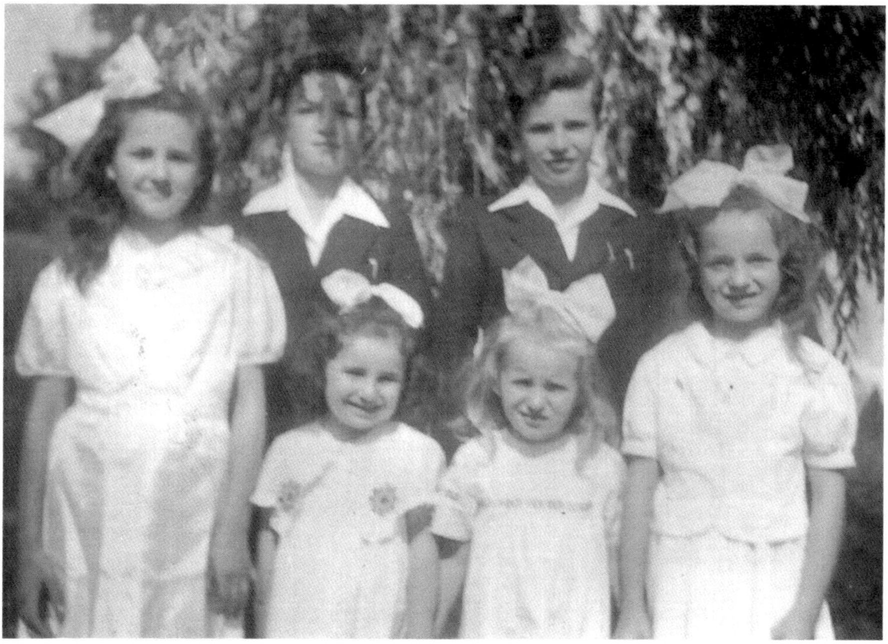

quickly, found their American acquaintances to be patient and helpful and eager to welcome them into their games. Zenon and Luba spent their two months of school in 1948 as sixth graders and found that they were ahead of their classmates in mathematics. A teacher gave Zenon a lead role in a school play, taking advantage of his background. He was cast as a representative of the Russian tsar meeting with U.S. secretary of state William H. Seward to negotiate the sale of Alaska in 1867.

"I received a standing ovation by all the parents present for my loudly spoken lines of mixed Ukrainian and Russian," he said.

When time came for the students to sing at the school's graduation ceremony, Luba was unfazed that her grasp of English was causing snickers.

"The kids turned around and laughed because of my pronunciation, but that didn't stop me. I sang."

Meanwhile, little Irene—Lialia—was impatient because she wanted to learn. Back in Austria, she had taught herself how to read by asking her parents questions about the Ukrainian and German alphabets. And now Luba, who had adapted to a responsibility of being a second mother to Lialia, shared with the youngest child what she was learning in school.

"There was no holding her back," Lialia's big sister observed. "She was very independent. She never hung back and waited."

When Irene was older, she spent gift money on Nancy Drew mysteries. The family's stay in Colchester lasted only a few months. They moved in February 1949 to Philadelphia, where Father Izak was given charge of St. Josaphat's Church. During his brief tenure there, his children were introduced to movies and television. A theater was just across the street from their home, "and we saw every movie there was," Luba said. "I loved cowboys."

Luba and her sisters also fell in love with *Howdy Doody*, which they watched on a neighbor's television. Listening to radio and watching television and movies was helping the girls develop their English.

The three young sisters also began singing together, particularly tunes from the Disney movie *Snow White*.

"We all liked to sing, but Helen [formerly Olena] was the one with an ear," Luba said. They also took piano lessons. "Helen was excellent; Irene was good."

As for herself, Luba told her mother not to waste her money on lessons.

Their stay in Philadelphia lasted only ten months. In December, Father Izak moved to Holy Ghost Church in Brooklyn, New York. The family was still in Brooklyn two years later when their only American-born member, Nicholas, came into the world.

Up to that time, Irene had been "daddy's little girl," said an admittedly jealous Helen. Irene had been the youngest, but she was also the child born after Father Izak had rejoined his family in Ukraine.

"She would go to Dad and of course he would melt," Helen Ewasko said.

Come March 1952, as the family moved again, Nicholas had become the pampered child. The jealousy that Helen had felt did not pass to Irene.

"Irene was very happy," Helen said. "It looked to me like she really enjoyed having a little brother. And I did too."

The Izaks were returning to Pennsylvania, this time to Scranton. Another priest had asked Father Izak to trade parishes, and in accepting the change, he was finally finding a true home. St. Vladimir's Church became his parish for the next twenty-seven years.

"At Scranton, we got Americanized, especially Irene," Helen said. "Irene seemed to make friends easily."

The family's moves from city to city were not always with all the children under the same roof. Before the move from Colchester, Father and Mrs. Izak began sending their children away to school. Luba went to St. Basil's Academy for Girls in Fox Chase, Pennsylvania, while Andrew and Zenon were sent off to St. Basil's Prep School, in Stamford, Connecticut, which was conducted by Ukrainian priests.

"It seemed the best thing to do to send us away to school because the upstairs where we lived in Colchester was small," Luba said.

> *It was difficult for Mom and Dad with five little children. But I think also they were thinking of our education. The Sisters of St. Basil the Great were at St. Basil's, and Mom had had that order of nuns in Ukraine. I didn't feel like I was going to strangers. Besides, they knew Ukrainian and the Mass would be in Ukrainian.*

With wages of about fifty dollars a month, Father Izak was unable to assume the full cost of his children's education. His diocese and private donations helped, but the children were also assigned chores at their schools to pay some of the costs. They also had part-time jobs. At the conclusion of the school terms, unpaid bills remained, forcing Father Izak to take out a loan, according to Zenon.

In retrospect, Zenon would question the direction his parents followed in planning an education for him and his siblings. Their parents wanted them to have a Christian education, but they were already getting a sound Christian upbringing at home.

"Too many religion and theology courses may have been an overdose," he said, and may have deprived them of a wider spectrum of instruction that might have offered better opportunities.

As a daughter of a priest, Helen never really thought that her life was much different from any of her friends. But her father was home much more than her friends' dads, "so it was nice."

But that also meant he handled more of the discipline.

"I can't say that Dad was not approachable, because he was," Luba said. "But he was always busy, so we went to Mother when we needed something."

Back talk was not tolerated, good example was always expected, absence from any church functions was frowned upon and participation in daily family prayer in the home was without question.

The boys were their father's altar servers at Mass, and all of the children sang in the church choir.

Dating was an activity that the sisters would have to experience after their high school graduations, first because their father would not allow it and second because they were attending an all-girls school. Besides, the boys would shy away.

"I was not approachable until somebody got brave," Luba said. "I was not approachable because I was the priest's daughter."

Luba completed her high school education at St. Basil's, more than two hours from home, and Helen remained there through her sophomore year. Irene was allowed to stay home. Marywood Seminary in Scranton offered a setting where Irene would step from grade school to high school and then to college, all on the same campus.

The three sisters eventually were all at Marywood. After Luba's high school graduation, she enrolled in Marywood College, and Helen transferred from boarding school to the high school at Marywood.

Finally, they were together in the family home. Luba and Helen, still accustomed to ways of the "old country," were able to watch in the late 1950s and early 1960s as their baby sister adapted more readily to the lifestyle of an American teenager. She introduced slacks and blue jeans to the household. And Elvis Presley.

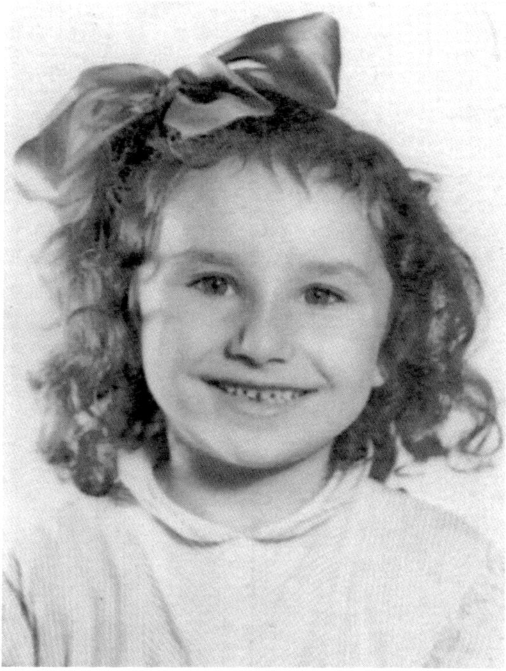

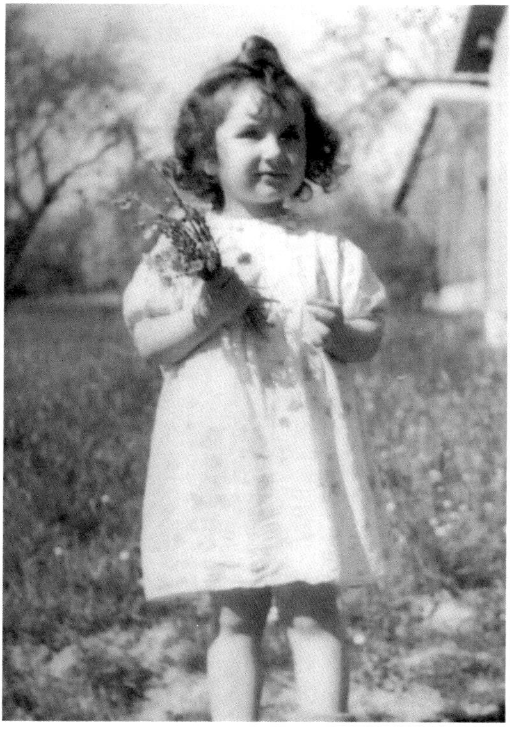

This page and next: Irene through the years. *Courtesy Helen Ewasko.*

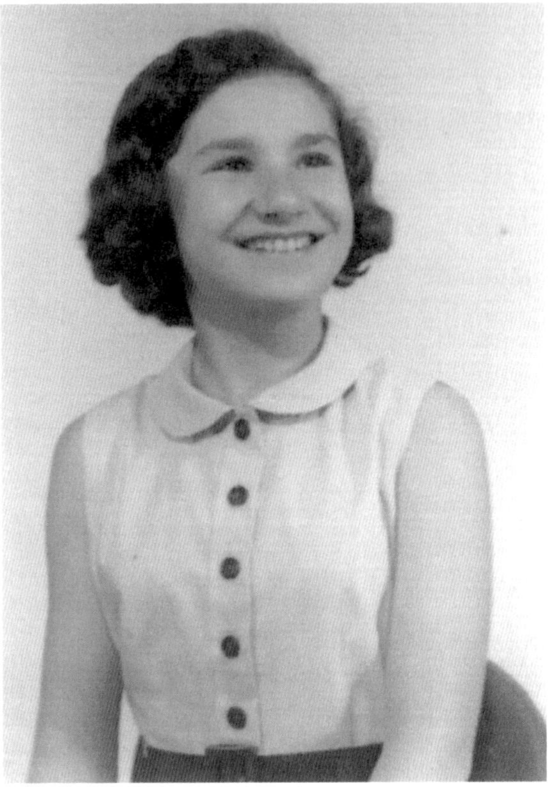

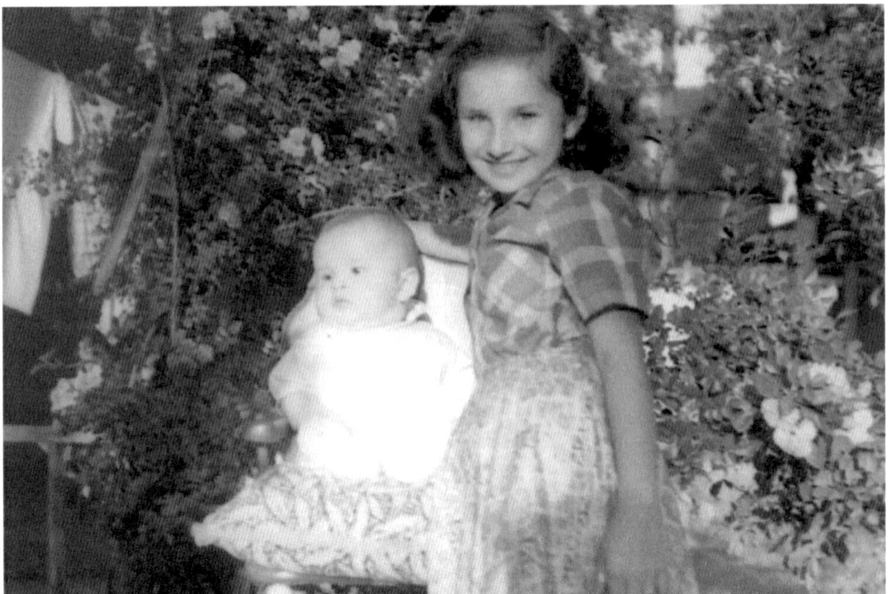

"That is something that my parents could not understand because Helen and I didn't go through anything like that," Luba said. "We were not exactly happy about it, either."

The family had a record player in the living room, and Irene was often seen leaning against the fireplace mantel, singing along with Elvis and sometimes dancing to his hits. Nick, growing up under the influence of his closest sibling and sharing her interests, was her occasional dance partner.

Later, Irene and Nick extended their common interests to the new rock group from England, the Beatles.

Andrew and Zenon loved to tease Irene about her new teenage eccentricities, but Luba, though not particularly enjoying Elvis, was quick to stand up for her baby sister. Bohdan and Maria Izak cast accepting but perhaps nervous eyes upon Irene's new fascination. Their discipline was less strict now. They realized times were changing, and they, too, had to adapt.

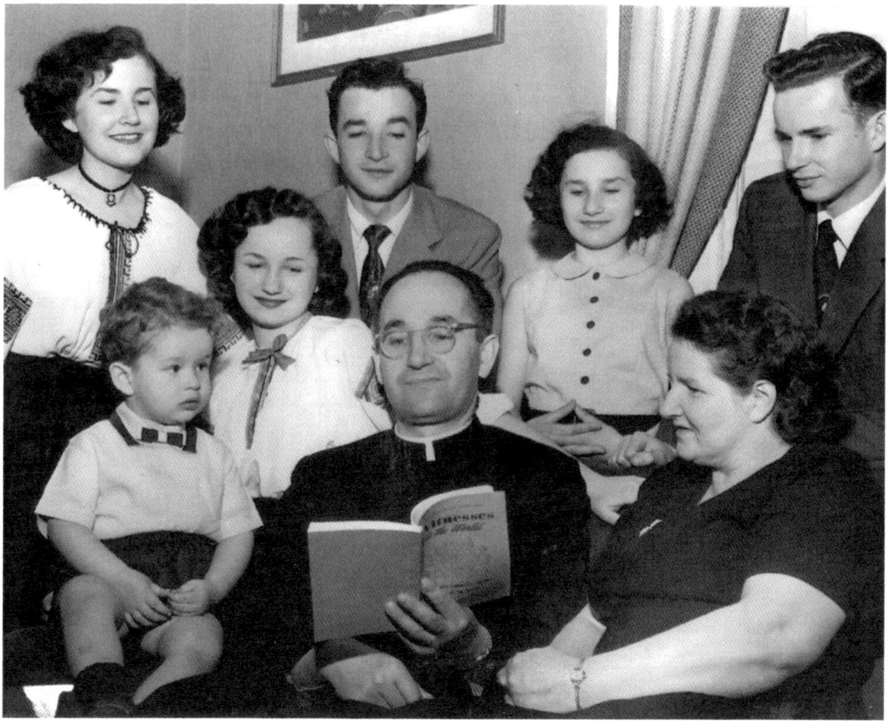

The Bohdan and Maria Izak family is shown on May 21, 1954, after all but the youngest, American-born Nicholas (front left), became naturalized citizens. From the left, at rear, are Luba, Helen, Zenon George, Irene and Andrew. *Courtesy Helen Ewasko.*

Irene, described by her sisters as a chatterbox who was always asking questions, excelled in school and made friends easily. In her eagerness to learn, she wanted to leave Scranton following her high school graduation, but she understood there was no money to send her to the more prominent colleges. She remained at Marywood, majoring in language, with her focus on French.

A classmate, Sonia Bednorchik from Binghamton, New York, remembered Irene speaking six languages fluently.

"She had a bubbly personality, was always smiling," Sonia said. "She was very trustworthy and always saw the good side of everyone. You enjoyed being in her company."

Boys were still hardly in the picture at this all-girls college, although Irene had a date for one campus "day hop." She certainly hoped to marry someday, Irene told her friend more than once.

Irene excelled at Marywood College, where for four years she was a member of the Slavic Club and was club president in her senior year. She graduated in 1963. Then she was off to New York State to teach high school French.

A DRIVE TO DARKNESS

Helen Ewasko was startled by the thought that crossed her mind as she chatted with her younger sister.

"I looked at Irene, and I'm thinking, 'You poor kid, some idiot is going to kill you.'"

That was on May 21, 1968, in Helen's home at Dalton, Pennsylvania. She would see her sister one more time, a couple of days later.

Helen's sudden thought was not without cause. Irene had just arrived after driving from Quebec, Canada, and she told her sister of an experience the night before while she was on the road. It had rained, and because the windshield wipers on her Volkswagen were not working properly, she had to stop somewhere near the New York–Pennsylvania border. While she waited out the storm, a drunken man approached and frightened her.

There was something else that bothered Helen.

"She wasn't herself," Helen recalled. "She wasn't happy and bubbly as she could be."

Irene seemed to be avoiding adult conversation. All she wanted to do before heading out to Cleveland to visit a friend was to play with Helen's children—Steve, seven; Christine, five; four-year-old twins Lisa and Kathy; and Greg, three.

Helen had been somewhat familiar with mood swings in her little sister, but this was different. She recognized that Irene was apprehensive about the grades that would bring her master's degree at Laval University in Quebec.

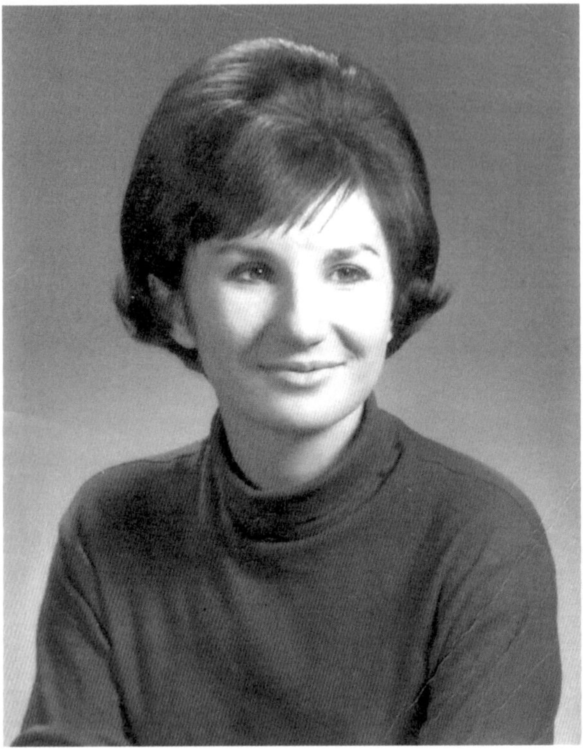

Irene Izak.

But Irene was also unsettled, uncertain about her future. And she was scarred from having been rejected by two men within a span of about seventeen months, two romances about which her family knew little.

Helen had not seen that much of Irene in recent times. While Helen was building a family, Irene had been away teaching, as well as attending Sorbonne University in Paris and, finally, the term she had just completed at Laval.

Irene's first job following her graduation from Marywood College was at Binghamton North High School in Binghamton, New York, teaching French.

"She was like a new breed of teacher, very interactive with the kids," said one of her students, Jacquelyne Schell of Watertown, formerly Jacquelyne Finch of Binghamton. "She was very passionate. She kept prodding. I think she was a little bit of a perfectionist. She wasn't satisfied for you to just get by. In her class, you walked in the door and you started working."

Irene never told her students about her background. "I thought she was French-Canadian," Mrs. Schell said. But Irene did tell of her eagerness to acquire a master's degree. Her students knew she would not be with them for long. Mrs. Schell recalled rare displays of moodiness in Irene, one of her favorite teachers.

"There was some quietness sometimes. It was noticeable because she was always so active. Her eyes would give her away, because they were so flashy."

Maxine Postle, who was one of Irene's first roommates in Binghamton, recalled having fun times with her. "We dated good friends together, but there were no serious relationships." After Miss Postle moved to Syracuse, she and Irene would talk of rooming together again if Irene got a job in that central New York city.

"She had a nice soft-spoken way about her," Miss Postle recalled, "but a big, contagious laugh for such a small person. She also spoke her mind, and if she didn't like someone or didn't want to do something, she said so."

During her last year in Binghamton, Irene appeared to be enjoying life less, according to another roommate, June Lawrisky Drake. They had been classmates at Marywood, and now they were sharing an apartment with two other women in Binghamton. Irene was becoming a loner, Mrs. Drake said. While her roommates went out, she stayed home. Toward the end of their time together, Mrs. Drake said Irene grew increasingly moody.

"I remember coming home one day and finding her sitting in the living room, staring into space. My last impression of Irene is that she almost didn't realize that anybody was there."

Irene's withdrawal may have been prompted by her finances and her goal for a master's degree. She spent the summer of 1964 studying at the Sorbonne in France. Her last job, for the 1966–67 school year, was at East High School in Rochester, New York. And then she attended Laval University in Quebec City.

"I spent all year scrimping, and I have just enough to live on," she wrote in October 1967 to her cousin Marie Kowalsky Lambrecht at Lake George, New York.

As children, Irene and Marie—Nusia in the old country—had been inseparable while their families fled from Ukraine. In Austria, they picked daisies together and made rings of the flowers to wear on their heads. They climbed trees to retrieve twigs and branches, the raw materials for their little moss houses.

When the Izak family immigrated to the United States, Irene was torn away from her cousin. The Kowalskys moved a year later, settling in Cleveland, and the two cousins renewed their sister-like relationship whenever their families managed rare reunions. As they grew older, they occasionally corresponded.

"I feel like a creep," Irene said in her October mailing because she had not been able to attend her cousin's wedding.

And then she revealed a romance that had developed in the summer of 1966, only to leave her heartbroken:

> *No one will probably come to my wedding, God, if I even have one. At the age of 25, one begins to wonder…I was madly in love with him* [so much that she passed up Christmas with her family so that she could spend the holiday at her beau's parents' home]. *And then he broke up with me. Well, let me tell you, it was hard.*

At Laval, she was love-struck again. And again, her boyfriend broke off the relationship. Irene told Helen only that the boy was from Ontario and that she was so depressed that she cut classes. Her friends came to her apartment to check on her welfare.

"I wanted to stay in Quebec," she wrote to cousin Marie on May 22, 1968,

> *but the presence of a boy I like, who dated me all year, but has a steady girl out west somewhere in Canada, has fixed that idea. I couldn't live there and not see him and it would be quite possible that he would never call and I've had enough of this pain.*

But she was not happy at home in Scranton, Pennsylvania, either.

"I come home and suffer because I have no one here to talk with," she told her cousin. "Laval was great. There were always people to do things with…Now it's zero. I guess I'm a bit disillusioned. Scranton does not do great things for my morale."

One of Irene's acquaintances at Laval, Maria Gailiusis, was from Cleveland, and she suggested to Irene that she do some job hunting there. After spending a few days with her parents, siblings, nieces and nephews in Pennsylvania, Irene packed her Volkswagen and, with little money in her purse, headed northwest to Cleveland. But her heart was still north of the border.

"All I want to do is go back to Laval," she wrote to her cousin, "and the boy I like doesn't want me. He sure pulled the wool over my eyes. Being dropped again by a boy I cared for makes me feel like not existing."

Irene started her drive from Scranton to Cleveland late in the day. Helen Ewasko asked her sister why she wanted to drive at night.

"I make good time at night," Irene explained.

Irene was not a particularly good driver, "made worse by her smoking and lighting cigarettes while driving," Miss Postle said. In the Scranton area, Irene had been injured in an accident, caused by her failure to observe an oncoming vehicle while she was making a left turn.

"She avoided making left turns as much as possible after that," Miss Postle said.

Irene was in Cleveland for a week, staying at the home of her mother's brother, Myron Kowalsky. She apparently did little job hunting, as one of her cousins, George Kowalsky, remembered her only "hanging around the house" and visiting relatives.

Toward the end of the week, she received a phone call. The conversation was in French, so the Kowalsky family only knew what Irene later told them.

The caller, Rosalie Banko, a Pennsylvania native who established her career in Quebec, said the conversation was in French at Irene's choosing. But in their days together at Laval, they had often conversed in French, she said. It was part of their learning process.

Miss Banko had called to tell Irene of a school district in Charlesbourg, Quebec, that was interviewing for English teachers. Since the interviews would likely end in June, it was imperative that Irene head back to Canada soon.

Nothing that her hosts in Cleveland said could dissuade Irene from leaving.

"I need a job right now and I'm not staying here for one," Irene wrote to Marie Lambrecht on Saturday, June 8, 1968. "I've wasted too much time here already. I want my freedom back, my old way of living."

She promised to visit Marie at Lake George following her interview in Canada but warned, "I have just enough money to buy gas for this long trip."

Perhaps it was that same night, according to family accounts passed on to Marie Lambrecht and Helen Ewasko, that Irene had her haunting nightmare. She screamed. Myron Kowalsky and his wife, Stefania, ran to their guest's room and found her crying and holding her head. They asked what had happened to so upset her.

"Somebody was hitting me on the head."

It may have been a recurring dream. Zenon Izak recalled an earlier, similar nighttime experience under his parents' roof in Scranton.

"Terrible screams came from her room. I rushed to her room, as did mom and dad, and she was sitting up in her bed, all sweaty."

Her brother did not remember what the nightmare was about.

Late Sunday morning, George and Russell Kowalsky washed their cousin's car, helped pack it and gassed it up for her. That afternoon, George escorted Irene out of the metropolitan area, seeing her for the last time.

Her next stop was Rochester, to visit one of her former roommates, Virginia Fitzmaurice. She arrived at about 9:00 p.m. on Sunday, June 9, and stayed little more than an hour. Miss Fitzmaurice urged her to stay the night, but Irene told her she would be staying with her friend Maxine in Syracuse. She would resume her drive to Canada on Monday, she said.

Maxine Postle was expecting Irene, but as Irene drove the approximately ninety-minute stretch between Rochester and Syracuse, she changed her mind. Her eagerness to reach Canada, and her fearlessness about driving at night to make good time, prevailed. She called Miss Postle with apologies. She would not be stopping.

After exiting the New York State Thruway at Syracuse, Irene followed the signs to the route that she had taken before on her trips between Scranton and Laval, heading north on Interstate 81.

She enjoyed music. As the miles passed, the VW's radio entertained. Perhaps she searched the dial, hoping to hear Elvis again, maybe the Beatles or another of her favorites, Barbara Streisand.

The radio would not allow her to escape the news of recent days. Five days earlier, on June 5, an assassin's bullet had taken down a presidential hopeful, Senator Robert F. Kennedy, in Los Angeles. On Sunday, according to a news report, the senator's widow, Ethel, pregnant with their eleventh child, joined thousands of mourners at Arlington National Cemetery. Soon, the political campaign would be heating up again as the nation readied to replace President Lyndon B. Johnson, who had chosen against seeking another term. Richard M. Nixon and Hubert H. Humphrey were the top runners for their respective political parties.

Another recent assassination was still being updated. James Earl Ray, charged in the slaying of Dr. Martin Luther King Jr. on April 4 in Memphis, had been hauled into court for added charges.

The war that was tearing Irene's adopted country apart and undermining Johnson's presidency was continuing to claim American lives in Vietnam. The Viet Cong were shelling Saigon for a tenth consecutive day, a radio reporter quoted from the wire service.

And Jimmy Brown, the retired professional football star, was arrested Sunday, accused of assaulting a woman.

Irene couldn't care less about what the sports report offered. The New York Yankees had been struggling, but perhaps there was hope with their double-header win the day before over the California Angels. Out on the West Coast, Don Drysdale of the Los Angeles Dodgers was setting a new record with his string of consecutive scoreless innings pitched.

About five miles after passing Watertown, Irene stopped at a rest area to use a pay phone. New York State Police later traced the call—her last—but have not disclosed whom she contacted.

Soon after she left the rest area, Irene made an unscheduled stop. She noticed a dark blue car coming up fast behind her and then observed that the driver pulled alongside. As was customary for a trooper in an unmarked car attempting to halt a female motorist, Trooper David Hennigan turned on his car's dome light and placed his Stetson on his head. Irene, recognizing this to be a state trooper, promptly pulled onto the shoulder of the highway and stopped.

Trooper Hennigan advised his headquarters at 1:50 a.m. on Monday, June 10, that he had halted a tan Volkswagen, bearing New York tag number 3W-4620. He greeted the small-framed motorist and told her that she was speeding at about seventy-five miles per hour, ten miles per hour above the limit, according to investigators in the case.

The trooper later told investigators that he inspected her license and vehicle registration, questioned her about where she was from and where she was headed and then sent her on her way with only a warning that she watch her speed. One of his colleagues found this uncharacteristic of Trooper Hennigan.

"He was a paperhanger," said former trooper David R. Fleming, who was also on patrol that night. "He wrote a lot of tickets."

Because of that, his shift commanders granted him liberal use of the concealed identity car, Fleming said.

Trooper Hennigan did not delay Irene long, but she had no choice but to watch her speed. The trooper possibly remained within sight much of the way as she proceeded the remaining sixteen or so miles to the American span of the Thousand Islands Bridge, located about midway between Clayton and Alexandria Bay, New York.

As Irene made her last stop on the United States mainland at 2:09 a.m. to pay the bridge toll, she watched the trooper's car as it was about to crest the bridge. She appeared to be nervous, toll collector Clifford F. Putnam, a sixty-three-year-old retired Watertown cop, later told police. She took out a cigarette and asked the toll collector for a light, even though police would later find that she had plenty of matches in her purse.

As Putnam gave her a light, he noted that the woman's hand was shaking. Irene pointed out the unmarked car just as it was about to disappear beyond the peak of the bridge and asked the toll man why state police would stop a car without reason in the middle of the night. Putnam rationalized that there had been some burglaries in the area recently, so perhaps troopers were monitoring traffic.

After resting for about a minute at the tollbooth, Irene continued on her way, taking the bridge to Wellesley Island. The north rim of the bridge took Irene onto a two-lane, tree-lined road that led to the Canadian span five miles away. Along the dark road were a few summer cottages and a state park serving campers, boaters and fishermen; there was also a tavern.

She drove up to a pull-off along the road, bordering DeWolf Point State Park, just a mile from the bridge to Canada's Hill Island. Police could suggest no logical reason for this stop. From her previous trips, Irene knew that public restroom facilities were available at Canadian customs. She had sufficient fuel in the car, police would later determine, and no mechanical problem in her VW was found.

But she stopped and parked at a location that a former cop called "the loneliest place on earth" on a cloudy, pitch-black night. Irene was about to carry to her grave her reason for stopping.

She encountered a person. A bruise later found on her face indicated that she might have initially been struck there. Then came a blow to the back of her head, stunning her, perhaps killing her instantly.

The attacker dragged her over guardrails and down into a grassy ravine. There, Irene's head was pummeled with several rocks that lay in reach of her killer.

By all appearances, the killer was in a rage.

At 2:35 a.m., Trooper Hennigan radioed his headquarters, reporting that he had discovered a body over an embankment, apparently a homicide, "possibly a female."

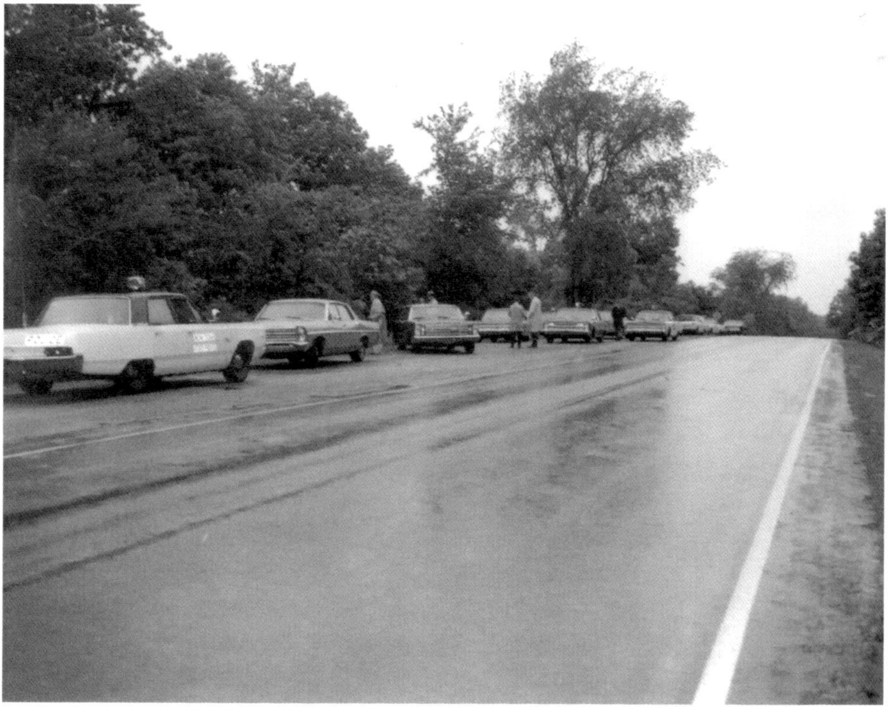

New York State Police cars lined the rest area adjacent to DeWolf Point State Park on June 10, 1968, following the murder of Irene J. Izak. *Courtesy* Watertown Daily Times.

State police investigator Raymond Polett, remembering three decades later what Trooper Hennigan told him, repeated the officer's account:

> *I was heading north, and I saw this Volkswagen parked, also pointing north, just off on the shoulder. I recognized it as the same Volkswagen I had stopped earlier, down by Watertown. Driven by a white female.*
>
> *When I saw the car parked there, I stopped. The car was empty. The inside light was on. The headlights were on, and I started calling out to her. I got no response. I started looking around, and I saw the body down over the bank. I went down, checked the body, and came back up and called Watertown. Then I went down to the body again.*

Sergeant Gerald DeGroot, manning the desk at the Watertown headquarters, dispatched his patrols to the island. Troopers David Fleming and Ronald Amyot, who were about fourteen miles away on Interstate 81 when they heard the sergeant's command, were first on the scene. Trooper Fleming said they met no southbound traffic while en route to the scene, so he was hopeful that the killer had not crossed to the mainland. Trooper Fleming pulled up to a widened section of road where he found a concealed identity police car parked behind a Volkswagen. Then he saw Trooper Hennigan kneeling beside a body.

"What the hell are you doing?" Fleming asked his colleague.

"Who's there?" Hennigan called back.

"Fleming," he answered.

"We have a murder," Trooper Hennigan shouted.

Trooper Fleming told his rookie partner, Amyot, to take their patrol car back to the American span and close off traffic. Then, Trooper Hennigan said he heard something, so he and Fleming went searching in the woods.

Trooper Peter J. Burns, who had taken the radio call while just north of Watertown, pulled up minutes later. He saw neither of the other troopers, since they were doing their search.

Trooper Burns called out, drawing a response from Hennigan.

"Who's that? I think I heard something."

After Burns asked about the whereabouts of the body, he said Hennigan emerged from the woods and pointed to the corpse with his flashlight.

"I saw her. There was a lot of blood, and blood on rocks, too," Burns said.

And there was blood on Trooper Hennigan's uniform, which he explained was transferred from the woman's body when he checked her for signs of life, according to Polett.

Trooper Hennigan should not have touched her body, said David Fleming, "not until the BCI got their pictures of it. No way. I wouldn't have touched it."

As more troopers arrived, the island's north exit was closed, but that was about twenty-five minutes after Trooper Hennigan's call to Watertown, according to *True Detective* writer Jay Ettman.

Coast Guard craft began circling the island to monitor any boating traffic and watch for suspicious activity on the shoreline. Ontario Provincial Police started checking traffic exiting Hill Island, although it was probably too late to catch a killer.

The call went out for investigators assigned to Watertown and troop headquarters at Oneida, New York. Troopers began a house-to-house canvass throughout the sparsely populated eight-thousand-acre island.

When he got a chance, Fleming said he went back to talk to the toll collector who had met Irene so briefly during the night.

"He said he [Hennigan] scared the hell out of her, that he scared the hell out of her down on 81," Fleming said.

Fleming found that curious because earlier, back at the murder scene, Hennigan had said nothing to him about stopping the woman on the interstate.

Investigators sealed off the crime scene that morning and began a painstaking search for evidence, while other officers had the unenviable task of notifying the victim's family. But in Scranton, before notification was received, Bohdan and Maria Izak already had notions that something was wrong. They awoke with a strange uneasiness about Irene, and they went to the priest's church, St. Vladimir's, to pray that Irene would have a safe journey.

Investigators at Binghamton visited the home of Irene's sister and brother-in-law, Luba and Steve Boyko, to break the news and to ask some questions about the victim.

Steve Boyko telephoned his brother-in-law, Paul Ewasko, so that Irene's other sister, Helen, would be given the tragic word by a loved one. And Mr. Boyko telephoned a Byzantine Rite priest, a friend of Father Bohdan Izak, asking him to notify Irene's parents. Late in the morning, Father Izak could only hope that a horrible mistake had been made. He telephoned his brother-in-law's home in Cleveland. His nephew Russell took the call.

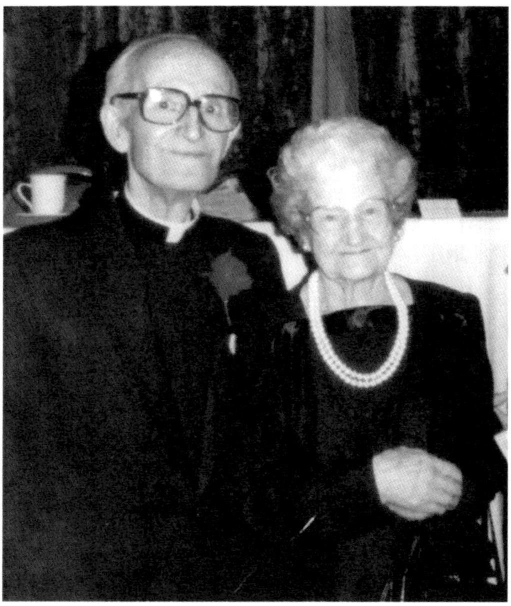

The Reverend Bohdan Izak and his wife, Maria, parents of Irene Izak. *Courtesy Helen Ewasko.*

"He asked if Irene was still here," Russell said. "His voice was very emotional."

When Russell gave the response that Father Izak did not want to hear, "he hung up on me."

Steve Boyko was asked by state police to identify the body. Accompanied by a friend, he drove to the Watertown state police headquarters. Before he was taken to see the body, he was questioned about Irene's activities and habits as investigators groped for clues of a possible motive.

He was then driven quickly to the county morgue at Watertown's Mercy Hospital. Upon arrival, one of his escorts asked, "Are you going to be all right?"

Affirming that he was, Steve was led into the morgue by the troopers and up to a covered body.

"They looked at me, and this guy grabs me around an arm, the other guy grabs me on the other arm. I looked at them both, and one says, 'Just a precaution.'"

Steve Boyko had no doubts about whose body he viewed that day:

> *I saw that face when it was alive, and I saw that face when it looked scared. The look on her face was a really frightened look. Her face was cleaned up but you could see where the bruising was, on her face and on her head. There was no mistake. Her face was beat up…it was beat up. There was no doubt who she was. No doubt. No doubt.*

Later in the day, Father Izak rode with an undertaker from Scranton, arriving in Watertown to claim the body of his beloved Lialia.

Before heading home, he asked to speak to the trooper who had last seen his daughter alive, according to Zenon George Izak.

"He refused to speak to Dad, no matter how much Dad pleaded," the priest's son said. "The other officers present all made excuses for Hennigan's absence. Dad was really frustrated and helpless in his efforts. He told me so."

INVESTIGATION TO NOWHERE, PART I

A telephone call at about 2:30 a.m. was almost second nature to thirty-six-year-old Raymond O. Polett. The Hackensack, New Jersey native had been a New York state trooper for a decade, and as an investigator over the last six of those years, he was accustomed to predawn calls to crime scenes.

But the call on June 10, 1968, was to haunt him for as long as he was a cop and into his retirement years.

Although he had once dreamed of being a New York City cop, Polett ended up taking a police job that placed him far to the north, a good six-hour drive from New York City, in an area where murders were few and far between. If Jefferson County experienced three murders in a year, it was a busy year.

He had been involved in one prominent case, on New Year's Eve 1964, when the death toll was three. Two brothers and the wife of one of them were shot gangland style at a rest area off Interstate 81, just north of Watertown. State police made three arrests in the case, but a grand jury indicted only one of the suspects, and that person was awaiting trial as Polett was being summoned to Wellesley Island to the scene of a woman's murder. The motive for the triple murder was the alleged involvement of the victims in a stolen-property ring. Police have since referred to the location of the shootings as the Egan rest area, named for the victims.

As Polett arrived at the location on Wellesley Island where Irene Izak had been murdered, he found one of his colleagues in the Egan case, Investigator

Charles C. Donoghue, already in the early throes of this new investigation. He also saw three uniformed troopers standing in a rest area overlooking the death scene, awaiting the arrival of investigation teams. David Hennigan was there with Peter Burns and David Fleming, who had returned after other troopers took up his position of closing the exit to Canada.

Polett was acquainted with Trooper Hennigan, since both men had been state police officers in the Watertown area for a few years:

> *Dave was sort of a flamboyant-type guy. He was a bit loud. You could hear him all over the barracks when he was talking. He would joke around a lot. Not unpleasant to be around. He was a bit of a BS'er, I think.*

Parked in the rest area in front of Trooper Hennigan's unmarked police car was a Volkswagen, its headlights still on, with the front wheels turned slightly to the left, as if the driver had started to pull back onto the highway. The rest area was wide enough to accommodate three cars parked side by side, but the Volkswagen and the police car were parked just off the edge of the road.

The driver's window in the Volkswagen was rolled down about four inches. There was no body damage on the car, possibly indicating that it had not been forced off the road by another vehicle.

Inside the auto, clothing and other items were in "general disarray," Polett said, but it did not appear that the car had been ransacked. "It was just a matter of, I think, a girl who wasn't that particular about packing her clothes and stuff," he said.

The victim's small green suitcase rested on the rear seat floor, along with a black raincoat, a blue scarf and other apparel.

Of particular interest to the detectives was the woman's snap purse, found open and resting between the bucket seats. Inspection of the handbag revealed the woman's wallet, some loose dollar bills, personal items, matches and Kleenex. A woman wouldn't leave her car without taking her purse, Donoghue observed.

"Somebody grabbed her and pulled her out of the car," he said.

A pair of women's eyeglasses was found on the ground at the rear of the Volkswagen, behind the left wheel.

Trooper Hennigan, "a little excited, as one might be," Polett said, led the investigator to the guardrails alongside the rest stop and shone his flashlight

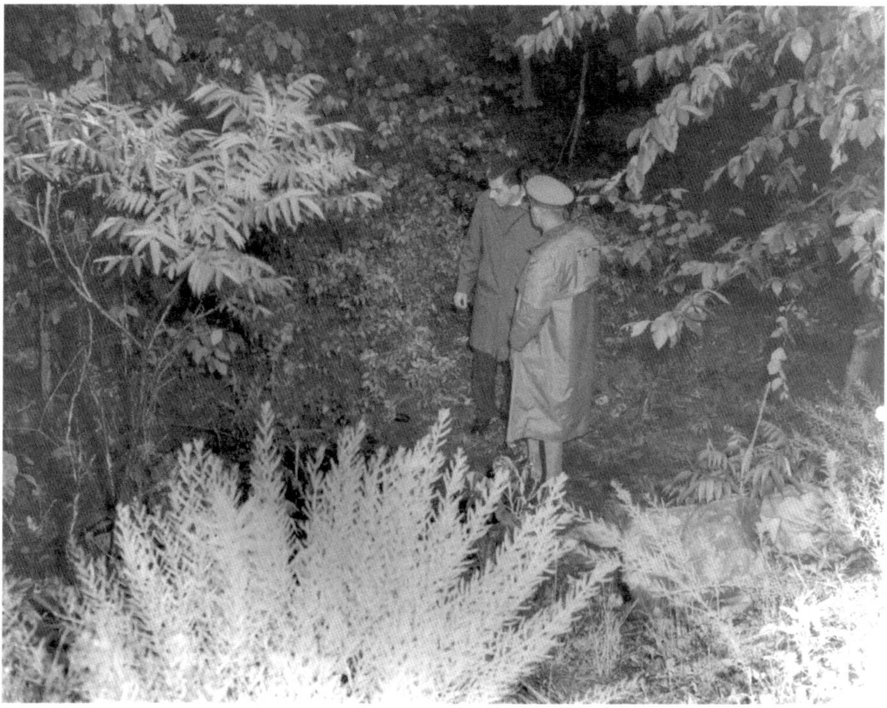

Ray Polett and another state police officer inspect the murder scene. *Courtesy* Watertown Daily Times.

down into the bushes, grass and weeds that lined a ditch.

"I had trouble seeing it at first because of all the vegetation and the fact that the upper part of the victim's body was clothed in a dark jacket," Polett said. "Hennigan pointed it out to me two or three times and I had difficulty recognizing what I was looking at."

This bothered Polett because Hennigan had told him he first saw the body from where the two men were now standing. If Polett wasn't able to make out what Hennigan was trying to show him, why had it been so easy for the trooper to find the victim?

Polett finally saw the woman's sandals. Then he saw the woman's body facedown, driven two or three inches into soft soil. He said he approached the body carefully, hoping to avoid trampling over evidence, "though it had been trampled by earlier arrivals."

The first trooper there should have approached the body to check for life, "but if you're investigating a crime like that, you take a circuitous

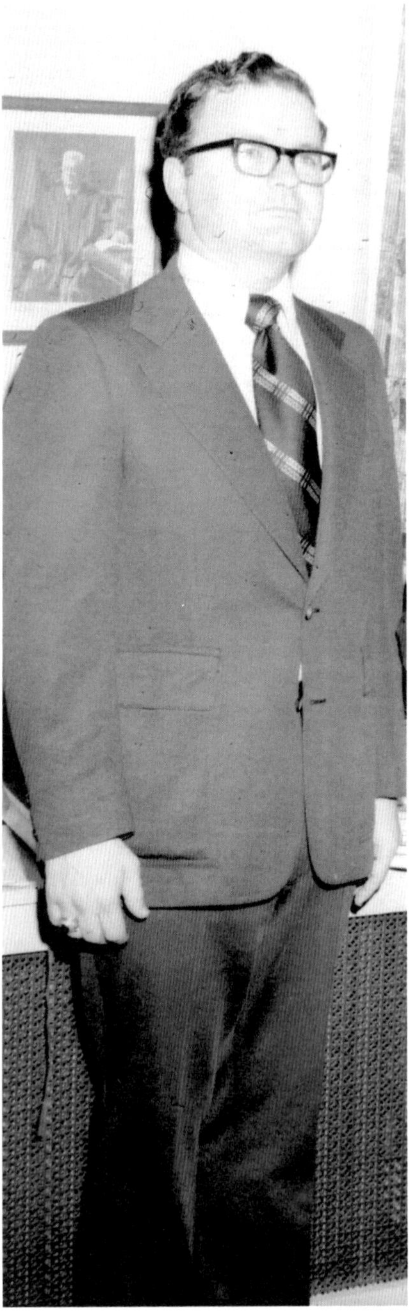

William J. McClusky, Jefferson County district attorney at the time of the murder. *Courtesy* Watertown Daily Times.

route," Polett said. "You approach and leave by the same route so when the identification people get there, you can tell them where you walked so that they aren't chasing, say, a hair from your head or a footprint from you."

When Polett began training to be a state trooper at a police academy in a YMCA at Troy, New York, "you were taught to protect and preserve the crime scene," he said. Certainly, that same training was still in place in 1962, when rookie Trooper Hennigan began his instruction.

"But it was also a reactive-type thing," Polett said in defense of a young officer discovering a body.

One or two troopers were not the only people to contaminate the murder scene, however. Darkness had not yet lifted when Jefferson County district attorney William J. McClusky arrived. At thirty-two, he had been the county's chief prosecutor about a year and a half. In another eighteen months would come his greatest disappointment as DA, an acquittal for the lone defendant in the Egan case.

As McClusky pulled up to the Wellesley Island rest stop, he observed that troopers were "having a fit" because the assistant medical examiner, Dr. William C. Heady, was going down to the body "against procedures," before evidence experts had arrived to examine the scene.

Polett had made a cursory inspection of the death scene and saw routine highway trash, such as beer cans, but he also noticed near the body five or six bloodstained rocks. One weighed about thirty pounds, he said. He saw hair and tissue on two of the rocks. The killer had struck with one rock, dropped it and then grabbed another and another to continue the assault. The killer was perhaps using fresh weapons to avoid getting the victim's blood, tissue and hair on his hands, Polett surmised.

"It looked like the motive was panic," McClusky said, considering where and when the crime occurred and how the victim was repeatedly struck on the head.

The majority of wounds were to the back of the skull, Polett said, but a bruise to the face suggested that the initial blow may have been rendered while Irene and her attacker were standing alongside the road, probably behind her car, where the eyeglasses were found.

When the eyeglasses were later placed on the dead woman's face, they were a snug fit, indicating to Polett that they had not fallen off easily and had probably been knocked off during a struggle.

Another indication of a roadside scuffle was found later when the victim's clothing was examined in a state police lab, Polett said. Photographs taken at the murder scene showed a white residue on the back of Irene's jacket, something that had not been visible to the naked eye. This was oxidation, Polett said, a transfer of material from the guardrails overlooking the ditch.

Polett's theory: "She was dragged or carried over the guide rails. It was on the back so that it was nothing that she could get on there by herself."

The victim had clung to her car keys, it appeared, unless the killer, as an afterthought, had placed them near the body.

As Polett continued his interview of Hennigan, hearing the officer's account of how he had met the woman back on the mainland, the investigator observed blood on the trooper's uniform.

"It looked like blood splatters, small droplets of blood, on his shirt and a larger spot of blood on the, I believe it was the right bicep area," Polett recalled three decades later without benefit of his investigation notes. "It could be the left bicep area. I guess a larger smear or blot of blood."

Trooper Hennigan explained that while checking the body for life, as he rolled the body over, the victim's head had rested against his upper arm, transferring her blood to his uniform.

"That was one of the things that made my eyebrows go up," Polett said.

> *Hennigan had been a corpsman in the army, so he would know better than most of us the proper way to handle an injured body, and I think that was*

done with some reckless abandon. You just don't take a person that obviously had apparent head injuries and just roll them over, even though there was a possibility of first asphyxiating. The head could be taken from that position without rolling the whole body over.

Polett and Donoghue both asked the trooper about his activities leading up to his discovery of the body.

The night had been slow. Since coming on duty at 11:00 p.m. Sunday, Trooper Hennigan had stopped only one car: Irene's Volkswagen. He reported that the encounter occurred about three miles north of Watertown, near the Egan rest area. After he let the woman proceed without a traffic ticket, he said he proceeded north, following the highway all the way to the Thousand Islands Bridge. After crossing the span, he said he took a turn to head west for routine patrol of the tiny island communities Fineview and Thousand Island Park.

In the summer, vacationers and seasonal residents populate the island, but the majority of those people are gone once cold weather arrives, leaving unattended homes as easy prey for burglars. State troopers routinely checked the deserted areas for suspicious vehicles, Polett said, but that detail was the responsibility of the Alexandria Bay station, not the trooper on interstate highway patrol.

David Fleming, who was also on interstate patrol, concurred. "He had no more right to be there than I did."

His swing to the west completed, Trooper Hennigan backtracked, but instead of heading over the bridge back to the mainland, he drove north on the I-81 extension toward the Canadian span of the Thousand Islands Bridge, he told investigators, according to Polett. After he passed the entry road to DeWolfe Point State Park, about a mile from United States Customs, he said he came upon the pull-off area where he found the Volkswagen parked with the driver's door open.

Later in the day, McClusky said he and an investigator rode the route with Hennigan, having the trooper show them where he had been on the island. Donoghue, thirty-six and in his sixth year with the Bureau of Criminal Investigation at Watertown, also covered the route separately with another investigator, Donald D. Marcellus. Their determination: it was possible for the trooper to have traveled his specified route of about nine miles and still discover the murder in the twenty-five or twenty-six minutes that transpired since Irene Izak was last seen alive at the bridge tollbooth on the mainland.

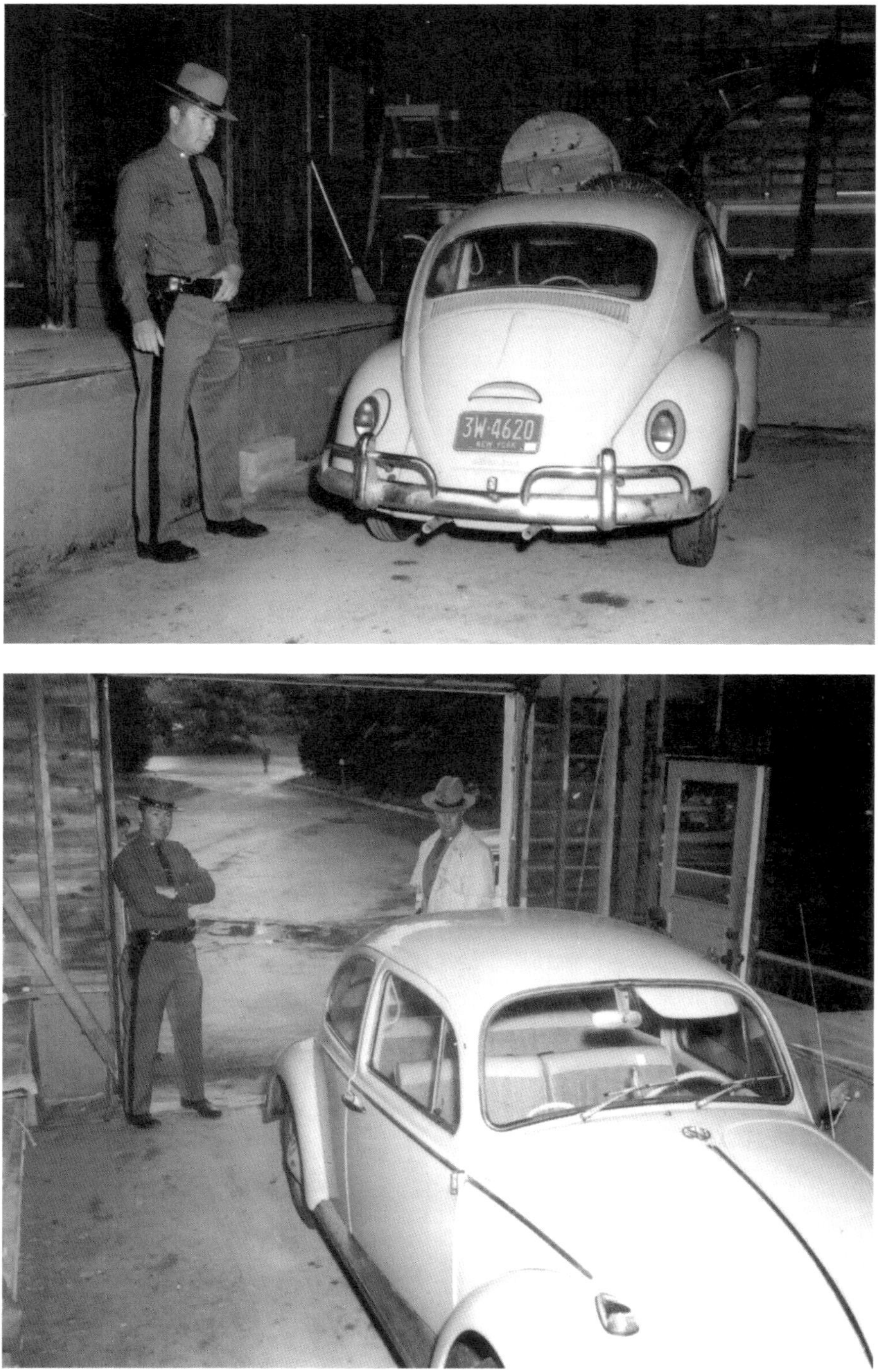

Irene's Volkswagen Bug, under state police guard as evidence. *Courtesy* Watertown Daily Times.

Donoghue also observed, however, that according to the trooper, Hennigan spent some of that time walking the length of the rest area—several car lengths—calling out for the owner of the VW before discovering the body.

Trooper Hennigan took two polygraph tests, but not before asking the district attorney if he should do it.

"I certainly would, especially if I didn't do it," McClusky told him. But then he warned the trooper that he should consult an attorney first.

A test was administered that same day at the Alexandria Bay station, according to Donoghue, who objected to the timing. The investigator insisted that Trooper Hennigan should be rested before taking a lie detector test, but other minds prevailed, he said. He remembered waiting outside the station for the examination to be completed.

The test "was flat," McClusky said. "They couldn't get a reading on him." Hennigan submitted to a second test, at a later date, and he passed, according to Donoghue.

The Volkswagen and Hennigan's police car were removed to the nearby U.S. Customs station garage to be dusted for fingerprints and scoured for other possible evidence. One latent print was recovered from the VW, state police disclosed years later. No match to friends, relatives, suspects or police officers would be found.

Soil samples were taken at the murder scene for analysis, and troopers paced the region in search of clues.

Only a few campers were found in the state park that bordered the murder scene. Their records were checked, and nothing unusual surfaced, Polett said. Many campers who had spent the weekend had moved out before Irene ever reached the area because the weather had been so cold and damp, Polett said.

A cold, drizzling rain, as described by Polett, may have denied evidence technicians a chance to find a possible telltale clue. At the top of the rear bumper of the police car, where it rounded toward the driver's side, was a "perfectly round" spot, about a quarter inch in diameter, he said.

"At least four people saw it," he said. "I saw it. And I have seen enough blood to know that it could have been blood."

But the spot disappeared.

"Before anybody had the foresight to preserve it," Polett said. "It got washed off, or wiped off."

Two bloodhounds were brought from Oneida, but the dogs were unable to develop a trail. Troopers went door to door on the island seeking suspects and witnesses. No buildings were in sight of the murder scene, but farther away lay some forty cottages. Only two occupants were found, and they had nothing to offer police.

If the killer had fled, he had only three immediate escape routes. To the immediate left of the road and rest stop towered an impassable twenty-foot-high sandstone cliff. A wooded area in the state park, and ultimately a riverfront, lay to the east. The highway's destination to the north was the international border, and given the small window of time, the trooper would likely have met a runner, or motorist, heading south.

No claim of such a sighting was offered. Meanwhile, personnel at United States Customs told police that only one or two vehicles had entered the island from Canada's Hill Island during the critical half-hour period. Back on the New York mainland, toll collector Clifford Putnam reported he saw seven or eight vehicles, including two lumber trucks, pass his booth toward the bridge between the times that he saw the woman in her Volkswagen and the sudden rush of state police cars.

Several vehicles had crossed the north border into Canada, Canadian customs reported. Two cars carried Canadian citizens, the border inspectors said; the others were travelers from the United States.

The *Watertown Daily Times* reported that two hitchhikers were questioned. One man, from Kingston, Ontario, who had been drinking, according to the *True Detective* story, was delayed on the New York mainland after he crossed the bridge several hours after the murder. The other, from Canton, New York, to the east in St. Lawrence County, was quizzed north of the border by Ontario Provincial Police, and he admitted that he had been "living off the rough" on Wellesley Island for a few days, the magazine reported. Police took their fingerprints for comparison and subsequently cleared them of suspicion.

A thirteen-year-old boy from one of the nearby river communities had run away from home for the weekend and was questioned after he returned on the day of the murder. Again, police found no cause for suspicion.

Another lead brought troopers to a mentally ill young man who lived within a mile of the crime scene.

"I remember interviewing him, but his time was well accounted for," Polett said. "He lived with his mother, and he hadn't left the house." The man had no history of violence, he added. "Hallucinating, primarily."

On the days that followed, state police conducted roadblocks to seek out regular island travelers, and requests were also repeated by news media for anybody who might have passed by some curious happening. A possible witness came forward.

A man was heading south, driving some boy scouts on a field trip, Polett said. The man told police he saw the Volkswagen and what he believed to be an unmarked police car parked behind it. The driver slowed down, but then the scout leader urged him to step it up and leave the area.

"Come on, get moving, I don't like this," was the witness's quote, as Polett recalled. "I just didn't like what I saw," the witness said. When Polett pressed the witness, the man guessed that he saw a state trooper having a rendezvous.

"That intrigued me," Polett said.

But there was also conflicting information from another passing motorist, who thought he saw three men standing around a dark-colored car parked behind the Volkswagen.

"I did not discount the possibility that Irene could be mistaken for a man if seen from the rear with the type of clothing she had," Polett said. "She did wear her hair sort of short. She had this sort of blousy windbreaker on and sort of baggy driving trousers."

But if it was a police car that this witness saw, "three people don't jibe," he said.

Donoghue said two waitresses who had gotten off work at 2:00 a.m. volunteered information. They said that as they headed home, going south on the two-lane road, they saw two cars parked in the rest area. The cars they described were the VW and a car matching the state police concealed identity car.

Donoghue was uncertain of the time of the women's sighting, only that it was between 2:00 a.m. and the 2:35 a.m. report by Hennigan of a homicide, "possibly a female."

Could Irene have been a "mule," a drug runner, and the victim of a deal gone bad? The question came up early, Polett said, since drug smuggling along the border was common.

"If she had been a mule, she would be someone on drugs," he said. But the investigation showed "nothing at all."

Polett and Donoghue took turns test-driving the Volkswagen. Polett said he could not get the car to go any faster than sixty-two miles per hour.

"And that's with my big foot on it all the way down to the floor…I was actually straining my foot on this little accelerator to see how fast I could have it go."

His partner had similar results. Both said the car was in fine running order.

During interviews with Irene's family and friends, police learned that she had made a call from a pay telephone not long before her death. The call was traced to a phone in a rest area on Interstate 81, north of Watertown and north of where Trooper Hennigan said he had made the speeding stop. The time of the phone call, compared to the time the trooper notified his Watertown command that he had pulled over the Volkswagen, showed a conflict in his report, Polett said.

Confronted with the new information, Hennigan changed his mind about where and why he had his initial meeting with Irene, according to Donoghue. The traffic stop, he conceded, was after her phone call and at a location closer to the bridge. No longer did Hennigan say the stop was for speeding, Donoghue recalled. Rather, the trooper said he had made a routine check on the car, just in case a crime such as burglary should later be discovered in the region.

Donoghue had another question. He said that when he first arrived at the murder scene that morning, Hennigan told him that he had not recognized the abandoned tan Volkswagen at the island pull-off. Yet Irene in her tan VW was the only motorist he had stopped during his patrol.

And Donoghue recalled his wakeup call that morning from Sergeant DeGroot.

"Hey Charlie, I've got a body for you on Wellesley Island. Hennigan just called it in. He says it appears to be a female."

Why, Donoghue wondered, was Hennigan now telling Polett that he immediately recognized the VW as that driven by the woman he had approached on the mainland?

Yet another issue puzzled Polett. When Trooper Fleming came upon the scene, Trooper Hennigan said he heard something in the woods, so both men began searching. Then Trooper Burns arrived, and Hennigan emerged to talk to him, leaving Fleming alone in his search.

"I thought that was really strange," Polett said.

> *You couldn't get me out of those woods with dynamite, not if my partner was in there. I would stay in there with him until such time as he came out or we gave up the search. You never risk your partner; you support each other all the way.*

Wanting to clear up these discrepancies, investigators decided the time had come to sit down with Hennigan for an interview. On a night when he arrived for his midnight tour at the Watertown station, he was ordered to report to Troop D headquarters at Oneida. There, he was taken into a room for questioning by Polett and Joseph F. Leary, a lieutenant in the state police Bureau of Criminal Investigation.

"I don't think we got that many answers," Polett said. "And we were only into the interview maybe a half hour, and Mrs. Hennigan entered the room."

Mrs. Hennigan had learned of her husband's sudden detail to Oneida, so she drove to the headquarters, arriving in the early morning hours. Identifying herself as a trooper's wife, she asked a desk officer where she could find her husband.

"Someone is in the back," the deskman replied.

"He no sooner got the words out of his mouth than she just went back in," Polett said.

There were no security locks to stop her.

The timing was crucial, Polett said. "I was very pointedly asking him if he was involved in the murder. He was denying it. He was denying involvement, and I'd almost consider it a routine interrogation at that time. He was emotional."

Mrs. Hennigan was also "quite emotional" when she entered the room, he said. "She accused me of picking on her husband, and I was supposed to be his friend. And then he got emotional."

Lieutenant Leary gave them permission to leave the room so that they could talk.

"And we really didn't get much farther than that; that's as far as it goes," Polett said.

He estimated the interview could have extended three or four hours had it not been for the interruption. Polett said he shares responsibility with Leary for not telling the desk officer that they were conducting an interview and did not want any interruptions.

> *You know, one or two in the morning and you don't expect to be disturbed. And people come and look at it in hindsight and say that you should have done this or should have done that. And I am the first one to quarterback myself and critique myself.*
>
> *But at that time, there was a certain amount of ill will, if you will; some troopers who just felt that we were picking on a fellow trooper.*

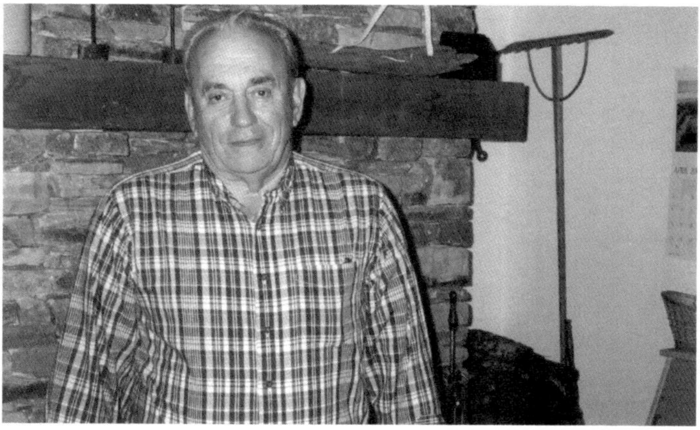

Ray Polett. *Photo by author.*

Certainly, they could have asked Mrs. Hennigan to leave, he acknowledged. "I am sure there would have been some friction, and if you are interviewing someone you don't want to further alienate that person perhaps by getting into a discussion with their spouse."

A friend of David Hennigan offered a different slant regarding that interview in Oneida. The Reverend Vincent T. Freeh, a former pastor at Our Lady of the Sacred Heart Church, Watertown, responding to a letter from Steve Boyko, expressed his views about the investigation in a letter dated February 27, 2000:

> *When David was being questioned, he had not even been allowed to call his wife. She finally showed up at the barracks demanding to see her husband. He calmed her down enough to get her to return home. He was then interrogated the rest of the afternoon and throughout that night, being released only on the following morning.*

He went on to say that Hennigan drove home after having not slept for two nights, dozed off and was awakened by the blast of an oncoming truck's horn. "Had he crashed, the newspapers would have seen that as a suicide and positive proof that he was the culprit."

Police never had another interview with Hennigan.

"He lawyered up," said Donald E. Brandstetter, an investigator stationed at Oneida at the time who assisted in the investigation. "His lawyer told us to charge him or get off his back."

Another police source disagrees, saying that Hennigan did not retain an attorney at that time.

Brandstetter's assignment was to interview the victim's family and acquaintances. He was sent to Scranton, then to Cleveland and finally to Quebec, where he needed a French translator.

Rosalie Banko, the woman who had telephoned Irene in Cleveland to tell her of a job opportunity in Quebec, said police came to question her on two occasions. She felt that police considered her a suspect because of the phone conversation that was conducted in French. She said she was advised by police that she and Irene's other friends in Canada should not attend the funeral. They were not pleased with the suggestion, but they complied.

Among the items found in Irene's car was a letter from her cousin Nusia, or Maria Lambrecht, of Lake George, New York. A response to that letter, the correspondence in which Irene said, "I guess I'm a bit disillusioned," arrived in the Lambrechts' mailbox on the day of the murder.

An investigator also arrived at the Lambrechts' door that day. From him, Maria learned of her cousin's fate. The family in Pennsylvania had not yet summoned the time, or the strength, to make all the notifications.

Since she was less than two months away from giving birth, Maria suspected that her aunt and uncle—Irene's parents—were trying to protect her.

After Maria gained control of her emotions, the officer at her door wanted to know if Irene had answered her letter. She handed over the freshly opened pages bearing Irene's handwriting.

Could she suggest why her cousin, traveling alone, would stop along a secluded highway in the dead of a damp and chilly night, Maria was asked. Would Irene have stopped to investigate suspicious activity or to help somebody who appeared to need help?

"To help somebody, maybe, but to stop and break something up that was going on illegally, she would never have done it by herself," Maria said. "She wasn't that foolish to do that."

And what if a stranger, perhaps a person in authority, had made a sexual proposition to Irene?

"She was a strong person in that respect," said Maria. "She wouldn't do it. No way. I know Irene wouldn't do it."

Learning about the victim is routine in any murder investigation.

"I got to know her very well," Polett said.

> *Extremely well. I would say in some cases better than the parents knew her. People would ask me a question about Irene at that time, and I knew*

> *a ton of things about her. I could answer a question just like that* [snaps his fingers], *to the extent of the kind of food she ate, the kind of candy she liked, the kind of movie she would go to, the kind of music she liked.*

Polett said she was not a "big party girl" but had a strong sense of friendship. And he was unconvinced by Mrs. Lambrecht's opinion.

"The thing that came to my attention most often was the fact that she would stop to help people," he said.

> *Would she have stopped on a cold damp night in a dark secluded area to pick up a hitchhiker or to assist a stranded motorist? I don't think she did, but she might have. I spoke with one girl who said she had been in a car with Irene when she pulled up to assist a guy who had trouble with his car.*

Polett found Irene's Canadian former boyfriend to be "a nice young guy, very complimentary about her. Nothing all that unusual."

The man in charge of the investigation on day one was Captain George J. Dana. On that same day, June 10, Dana had just taken over command of the Oneida troop's Bureau of Criminal Investigation, according to C. David Hudson, an investigator who several years later would inherit the case. Dana was doubtful about the suspicion being cast toward Hennigan.

"He didn't read it that way," Hudson recalls from firsthand knowledge.

The troop commander, Major Raymond D. Rasmussen, concurred with Dana, Hudson said, and both officers cautioned investigators against focusing on their one suspect. But Polett, Donoghue, Brandstetter and Hudson all deny that the two command officers "ran interference" to protect their trooper.

Polett said it was his duty to check out any possible lead, and he insists that he did. He traveled to a hospital for the mentally ill in Connecticut to interview a patient who was rumored to have been working in the Thousand Islands region at the time of the murder. This trip was prompted by a serial killer investigation in New Haven, where female victims had been bludgeoned with rocks.

"We don't want people to read into this more than is there," Polett told the *Watertown Times* in October 1970. But the New Haven murders were "similar, more so than others we have investigated."

The trip was unproductive. The administrator of the hospital refused to permit the interview.

"Nobody remembered his name," Polett said.

Again, this person also had no history of violent behavior.

The case became an obsession for Polett. On two occasions, he had a trooper drop him off at the scene so that he could spend the night in the woods to see if this was a regular walking route for somebody. All he saw was wildlife.

He carried Irene's photo.

"That was my reminder. I kept that in my car for a long, long time on the dashboard so that I would see it there all the time and it would reactivate my thinking about the case."

Donoghue said he did not need to carry Irene's photograph. "It was in my mind."

About fifteen months after Irene's death, state police received a ray of hope from police in Toronto, Ontario. A man jailed for a parole violation told one of his guards that he wanted to talk to homicide detectives about a murder. His subsequent written confession was vague and lacking details, but he told Toronto police "a story of killing a woman near the Thousand Islands International Bridge," the *Watertown Daily Times* reported.

Polett and Investigator Donald Marcellus drove to Toronto early in October 1969 to question twenty-six-year-old Albert Sinobert. The questioning lasted several hours. Sinobert had read the *True Detective* story about the murder, according to Polett. The only details he knew were contained in the story.

"The interview was generally unproductive," Polett told the *Watertown Times* upon his return from Canada. He and Marcellus were convinced they had interviewed a criminal who gets personal gratification from confessing to murders he did not commit.

Another motive for the apparent bogus confession: Sinobert wanted to move to an American jail, where he suspected he would receive better treatment, Polett said. Canadian authorities said the convicted burglar was being returned to prison and would be given psychiatric treatment.

Also in 1969, Polett drove to Michigan because John Norman Collins, dubbed the "coed killer," had been in the Thousand Islands region twenty-four hours before Irene Izak was murdered. In Michigan, Collins was charged in the deaths of seven women. But the detective returned home only to eliminate Collins, who was a week away from his twenty-first birthday, from their suspect list. Collins had left New York before Irene arrived.

> *Collins continued straight on to Massachusetts, and we verified all that. His time of arrival, what have you. Although he'd be an individual totally capable of doing something like this, we couldn't put him there. He wasn't there.*

Actually, Collins's modus operandi was different. He either shot, stabbed or strangled his victims while raping and sexually torturing them. Irene had not been subjected to such a horrid death.

Collins was given a life sentence.

A murder in southeast Jefferson County in January 1970 had state police looking at another possible suspect. Six-foot-seven James Leslie Simpson, twenty-seven, who had previously been confined in a mental health facility for molesting a girl, attacked a woman on a late afternoon on the main street of West Carthage, some forty miles from Wellesley Island. Betty B. LaForest, thirty-three, with a gaping wound in her neck, bled to death in minutes.

Rumors arose that at the time of the Izak murder, Simpson was staying in a cottage on Wellesley Island with a friend or relative.

"He was eliminated totally," Polett said. "As much as you want to identify a suspect, you just can't say that he was there when he wasn't. We found out that he had been spending a lot of time with his girlfriend out in Lyons Falls," in Lewis County, southeast of Jefferson County.

Another potential suspect surfaced in September 1972, after Watertown police arrested Arthur John Shawcross, twenty-seven, for the brutal slaying of an eight-year-old girl, Karen Ann Hill. The child died from strangulation and suffocation.

The arrest was made only hours after a search party of two Watertown cops and two troopers, including Hennigan, found the girl's body facedown under dirt and debris along a bank of the Black River in Watertown, beneath a bridge. One of the city officers, Augustine D. Capone, said he and his partner actually made the discovery.

"All of a sudden, the troopers were there," Capone said.

A few days later, using information provided by Shawcross, police found in a wooded area bordering the north edge of Watertown the remains of a boy, Jack O. Blake, a ten-year-old who had disappeared four months earlier. Shawcross spent fifteen years in prison after pleading guilty to manslaughter in the Hill girl's slaying. The plea bargain came back to haunt Shawcross's prosecutor, McClusky, in 1990, when Shawcross was identified as the serial killer of at least eleven prostitutes in Rochester, New York. A Monroe County judge gave him life in prison. The serial killer died in 2008.

In the Izak murder, Shawcross was just another dead end. That latent print from the VW was no match, and army records made available to state police placed Shawcross on military duty on June 10, 1968.

Shawcross was not the only serial killer to attract attention from investigators in the Izak homicide.

"We kept chasing down leads on possible suspects," Polett said. Prominent among those was Ted Bundy, who killed at least twenty attractive young women in the states of Washington, Oregon, Utah, Idaho, Colorado and Florida between 1974 and 1978. Bundy fed his evil passion by luring victims to his car and then bludgeoning them, offering an intriguing comparison to the murder of Irene Izak. But he raped and bit his victims, elements not present in the Wellesley Island incident. Ultimately, the investigation revealed that Bundy, twenty-two at the time, was in Colorado when Irene died.

Bundy was executed on January 24, 1989, in Florida.

District Attorney McClusky never presented evidence from the Izak case to a grand jury. The only evidence, he said, was circumstantial. He left office in April 1973 to accept appointment by New York governor Nelson Rockefeller to be a Jefferson County judge.

As the Izak investigation continued, Trooper David Hennigan remained on duty. Despite some harassment directed at him by the public, he was not given a temporary transfer, according to Polett. And despite appearances that he strayed from his assigned patrol area, gave conflicting details about his activities that fateful morning and may have erred in his murder scene actions, he was not suspended or otherwise disciplined, according to his contemporaries in uniform.

McClusky said he was told that disciplining Hennigan would have "looked bad for the troop."

Meanwhile, a television news reporter covering the Izak murder found state police to be particularly tight-lipped in this case. Joseph L. Rich was at the time in his second year with WWNY Radio and TV, located in Watertown. He had previously worked at another Watertown radio station, so he was experienced in dealing with the local troopers.

"It was a situation where Major Rasmussen and others from troop headquarters in Oneida were on hand and naturally took over the investigation, so everything had to be funneled through them," Rich said.

In other murder investigations over the years, there seemed to be a greater willingness either by the Watertown state police or the DA's office to more readily share information without jeopardizing their case. I think because of the sensitive nature of the investigation, much less information was shared. The way it was handled by the state police headquarters in Oneida did lend itself to journalists and others trying to sort out the facts for themselves regarding the murder, many of them thinking rightly or wrongly that it was a cover up.

Rich also said he found a piece of possible evidence at the murder scene and wondered what the police did with it. He said troopers allowed him to go down into the ditch after the victim's body had been removed, and he found a crumpled-up newspaper, an issue of the *Rochester Democrat & Chronicle*. He was certain he saw bloodstains on the paper, which bore the date of either June 9 or June 10, 1968.

"There was blood on that newspaper, and nobody can tell me differently," Rich said.

Had the killer taken the paper from Irene's car and used it to wipe blood from his hands or a weapon, he wondered.

Wanting to make sure the paper reached the proper hands, he took it to the state police headquarters at Watertown and there surrendered it to Major Rasmussen. "He thanked me and handed the paper to another officer."

No questions were asked, he said; nor was he fingerprinted, even though he had handled the potential evidence.

He asked a few days later if the paper proved helpful, and investigators "didn't know what I was talking about."

Three decades later, a retired Rasmussen would say he had no recollection of the stained newspaper.

As the years passed, troopers observed changes in their colleague David Hennigan.

But the changes were gradual. Before Irene Izak drove her Volkswagen into his life, Hennigan was called "Heathen" by his fellow troopers. The name stuck for a while, even after June 10, 1968, according to Fleming.

"He liked having that name, Heathen," Fleming said. "He enjoyed that."

Perhaps one of his character flaws leading to the name was that he had a temper.

"He quite often had tantrums," Fleming said.

Donoghue recalled the trooper's interest in pornographic magazines. He said Hennigan was known for going through trashcans in Interstate 81 rest areas in search of such material. On one occasion, Donoghue said Hennigan showed him his risqué findings. Fleming noted, however, that such behavior was not unique to Hennigan among the troopers.

In June 1979, Hennigan was injured in a bizarre accident. Operating an unmarked cruiser, he attempted to halt the driver of a decommissioned police car for speeding on a state road in southern Jefferson County, and a chase developed. As he reported by radio that he was falling back in the chase, the lead driver lost control on a curve and went down an embankment. The auto landed on its side, next to a creek.

Hennigan later reported that he did not witness the accident. His police car exited the highway at the same location, bounded down the hill, landed on top of the old cop car and then slid to the ground, also landing on its side. Two brothers climbed out of the other auto and assisted Hennigan from his vehicle. Both cars subsequently erupted in flames.

The trooper's injuries were listed as a neck sprain, cut lip and bumps and bruises.

Eventually, his colleagues noticed that Trooper Hennigan was beginning to show more interest in his Catholic faith, more so than they had previously witnessed. The beneficiary of his new involvement was his parish in Watertown, Our Lady of the Sacred Heart Church. In 1975, with the assistance of his two teenage sons, he built a chapel at the parish's Calvary Cemetery. He accepted no payment for his labors.

His motive was simple, he told the *Watertown Times*. The cemetery needed a chapel.

While continuing as a state trooper and also being active with his sons as a scoutmaster, he began training in 1977 for a role that was to set a new path for his future. Three years later, on October 4, 1980, a bishop in Ogdensburg, New York, ordained David Hennigan a deacon of the Roman Catholic Church. As such, he became a pastoral assistant at Sacred Heart Church. His duties included all church activities except the two privileges restricted to priests: celebrating Mass and hearing confessions.

For three years, he split his time between his two roles as Catholic Church deacon and state trooper. He concluded his road patrol work in September 1983, when he retired from a twenty-one-year career with the New York State Police.

A NIECE, A REPORTER AND A PI

She was only four, but Lisa Ewasko Caputo remembered the anticipation in spring and summer that her Aunt Irene, the schoolteacher in New York, was coming to visit. "She would bring us candy and gum. I remember pinwheels with little candies in the stems."

They spent time together in the backyard of Lisa's home at Dalton, Pennsylvania, sitting on a blanket playing with the Ewasko children's pet rabbits. "I also remember how pretty she was. I have memories of her skin complexion being perfect."

But the niece's clearest memory from her early childhood is of that day in June 1968, just as people of her Aunt Irene's generation recall what they were doing the day President Kennedy was gunned down in Dallas. Or like children of a later generation will not forget their whereabouts on September 11, 2001, when terrorism hit home in the United States.

Helen Ewasko was making ice cream cones for Lisa and her twin sister, Kathy, when Paul Ewasko made an unexpected early afternoon return home from work. With a strained look on his face, he sent the children outdoors so that he could speak privately with his wife. Soon after the girls had reached the driveway, they heard their mother's screams and cries.

Lisa does not recall what explanation her parents offered. "But I remember being confused and scared because my mom was so upset."

Soon enough, she would learn that her Aunt Irene was dead. Helen said she could not bring herself to tell the children that their aunt had been murdered. "I didn't want to tell them. They were too little."

Then came silence, years of silence.

When Lisa visited her grandparents, the Reverend and Mrs. Bohdan Izak, at the rectory of St. Vladimir's Ukrainian Catholic Church in Scranton, her eyes would invariably fall upon a painting of her Aunt Irene that hung on the dining room wall. She never heard any discussion about her lost aunt.

> *I remember always looking at it and feeling sad that no one really spoke about Lialia. I knew as I got older it was because no one wanted to upset my grandparents, but it always bothered me. Just as it always bothered me that no one pushed to find out about the murder investigation.*

Occasionally, she and Kathy snuck away for private moments in a closet, reading the *True Detective* story titled "Murderville—25 min. Ahead."

The pain of having had a daughter murdered was visible in Maria's and Bohdan's faces the rest of their lives. Luba Boyko said her father always blamed himself because, having been such a disciplinarian, he had given her more independence than he had allowed her older siblings. Father Izak cried that he should not have let her go or that he should have been with her. He often asked why, never coming up with an answer. Luba repeated the words that she had heard pass her father's lips so many times: "I want them to find out who did this. I would like to talk to him. I would like to ask him why. Why did he do it?"

Father Izak remembered the flight from the Russians and Nazis and pondered how his children could have been killed in the bombing at Bolotnia. Having come to the land of the free to feel safe, he asked how could he have lost his beloved Lialia in such a senseless, violent manner?

Father Izak made at least two trips to Watertown, hoping to learn something from Trooper David Hennigan, according to one of his sons, Zenon. About three months after the murder, Zenon and his wife, Christine, also made the drive into northern New York, but they met with the same dead end that had greeted the priest.

"Hennigan was not available," Zenon Izak said.

All that Zenon gained was a viewing of the site of the murder, courtesy of a state police investigator.

After years passed, with no answers to the questions of who or why, Helen said she raised a question to her father: "Daddy, how could they have covered up such a horrible crime?"

He did not answer, but eventually he echoed her query.

Maria was given a sedative after she was told of her daughter's murder.

"I wish they hadn't done that to me," Maria later told Helen. "I couldn't feel anything then."

Nicholas, Maria's youngest, remembered his father crying so much more than his mother.

Eventually, Father Izak dejectedly accepted that no answers were forthcoming from the New York State Police. Meanwhile, in 1984, Stephen Rubel, a private detective in Philadelphia, agreed to look into the case as a favor to a personal friend, Christine Izak, Zenon's wife.

That is when my interest in the case was stirred. By then, I had been a reporter for the *Watertown Daily Times* for thirteen years, and certainly I was aware of the unsolved murder that had occurred several hours after I had donned a cap and gown for commencement at Jefferson Community College in Watertown. Every time a murder occurred in Jefferson County, it was incumbent upon me, as police reporter, to remind our readers that this brutal killing of a young schoolteacher on Wellesley Island had still not been solved. Early in my career, I telephoned Bill McClusky, who was then still the DA, to ask him about the case. I did not know if I was hearing nervousness on the other end of the line; perhaps I was just unaccustomed to his mannerisms in dealing with reporters. But when I hung up the telephone, I was left puzzled about why my few questions had rendered no answers of any substance, just evasiveness.

Late in December 1984, Mr. Rubel called me, perhaps to pick my brain but mostly to get the word out that he was hoping to find somebody, anybody, who might give him some direction for his investigation. He said something that startled me, something that I don't think I had ever considered—or perhaps did not want to consider—and had not seen reported in any of the old news clippings about the murder.

Mr. Rubel said he believed the killer was the state trooper who had confronted Irene that night along Interstate 81.

I had met David Hennigan on the job and had, on rare occasions, gleaned information from him for news stories. He never came across as overly friendly, but I didn't sense any hostility.

There was one moment, however, that has always stuck with me. In my daily routine on the police beat, I made 6:00 a.m. stops at the state police station on Route 37, north of Watertown. Trooper Hennigan was on desk duty one morning, not long before his September 1983 retirement.

He was angry—about what I never learned—and he was showing it. As I walked in the door, I saw him throw something down on the desk and heard him shouting expletives. When he realized I was there, he quickly restored his demeanor, and two or three troopers who had been listening to this tirade promptly left the room.

Certainly, no cop is above such conduct, but it struck me because this man had been a Catholic Church deacon for close to three years. I can be accused of being naïve, but I didn't feel that what I had just witnessed was befitting a man who, at Sunday Mass, would be reading the Gospel and distributing Holy Communion.

I dared not report Mr. Rubel's suspicion in my *Watertown Daily Times* story, which appeared on December 29, 1984. The closest I came was quoting him: "The police didn't show the family anything they had…and the family was left thinking there was a cover-up."

The private detective cautioned me against calling Father Izak, because the priest had not been informed of his entry into the case. But somebody, a mystery caller, telephoned Father Izak and asked if he wanted the case investigated. The priest "made it very clear" that he did not and, without asking who was calling, ended the conversation, according to Paul Ewasko.

"He just did not want any more emotional pain than he and Mother already had," Mr. Ewasko said.

Mr. Rubel's involvement was short-lived.

From that time on, in deference to the ailing parents, all family discussion about the murder was quashed, Mrs. Caputo said.

Father Izak died at age eighty on December 28, 1988, in his home. He was buried at his slain daughter's side at St. Vladimir's Cemetery. Maria followed him to the grave three years later, passing on November 2, 1991. She was eighty-three.

Not long after Mrs. Izak's death, both Lisa Caputo and I, unaware of one another, began our separate searches for the truth. On my part, troubled by Mr. Rubel's comments, I contacted Christine Izak in 1993 with plans of doing a twenty-fifth-anniversary story. My disappointment at her respectful decline to cooperate sidetracked me, and the story fell by the wayside, perhaps like the state police investigation. I would learn later that Mrs. Izak's decision was out of concern for her husband and how he might react emotionally to reliving the events surrounding his sister's murder.

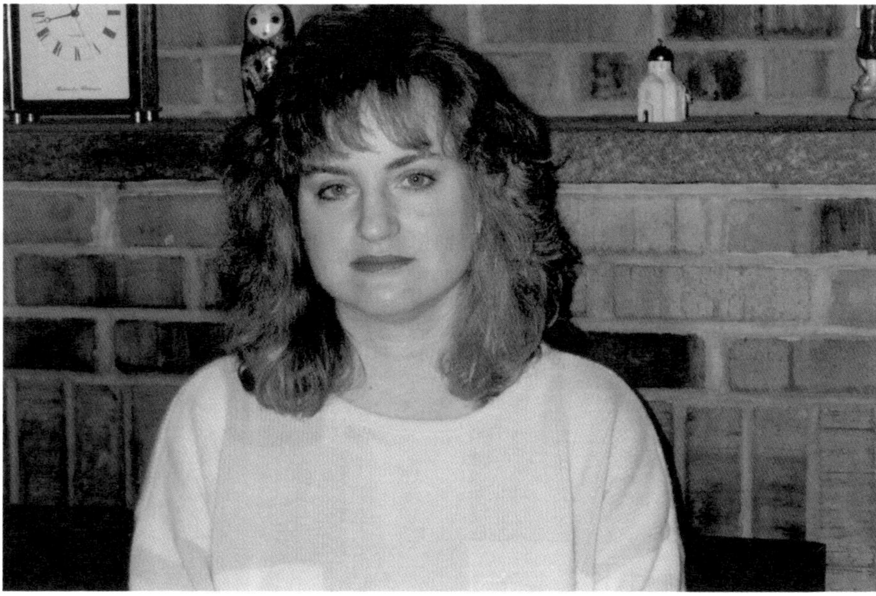

Lisa Caputo acted on her childhood memories to try motivating New York State Police to bring justice for her Aunt Irene. *Photo by author.*

Lisa, meanwhile, now felt that with her grandparents' passing, she was free to start asking questions. Her first question was to her mother, seeking permission to write to the New York State Police. That granted, she sent a letter in December 1994. State police responded but refused to release any information about the investigation. They agreed, however, to return Irene's Marywood class ring, which she was wearing on the morning of her death. Lisa asked that it be delivered to her at her workplace, PNC Bank in Scranton.

The ring arrived on March 3, 1995. A day earlier, she had learned that she was pregnant with her first child, so there was already excitement among her co-workers. "I remember the mail person bringing it right to me and my hands shaking. I opened the envelope, and the ring was inside this little plastic box."

She put the ring on and wore it home, later showing her mother. "It was a very emotional day," she said.

Lisa continued writing and telephoning officials in Albany and Oneida for the next three years but received little in return. On June 5, 1998, she mailed a letter containing a request under the Freedom of Information Law. She had a response in six days: request denied. Frustrated and angry, she tried the Internet the same day, June 11, posting notices on various boards seeking advice about what she might be able to accomplish under the Freedom of Information laws. The next day, her mail brought a surprise package from state police. Inside she found Irene's watch.

Although I had written nothing about the case in 1993, I didn't stop asking questions. The feedback I received from two retired state troopers, an active state police investigator and a retired deputy sheriff all cast suspicion on one man: David Hennigan. Additionally, another retired investigator, Charles Donoghue, initiated contact with one of my colleagues at the *Watertown Daily Times*, Larry Cole. Donoghue's message was the same: take a hard look at Hennigan.

My source within the state police, talking to me in strict confidence, explained the suspicious circumstances and conflicting stories involving Hennigan and expressed his hope that before he ended his career he would have a chance to confront the retired trooper. The opportunity never presented itself, however, and the investigator's retirement party has come and gone.

I became determined to write a thirtieth-anniversary story in 1998. I tracked down Ray Polett, who was finally taking retirement seriously in Auburn, Pennsylvania, after jumping from a state police career to being a sheriff in New York's Lewis County and, still later, police chief in the Philadelphia suburb of Upper Dublin Township. His frankness in telephone interviews about the jaundiced eye he directed at Hennigan fueled my interest.

Dutifully, I telephoned David Hennigan, hoping to ask him to reminisce about what had to have been the most memorable night of his police career and eager to get his reactions to Polett's statements. He declined comment and hung up.

Larry Cole continued his conversations with his source, and I again set out to make contact with the Izak family. My first call was to the home of Zenon and Christine Izak in Warminster, Pennsylvania. I was later told that when Zenon's caller ID device displayed Watertown's 315 area code, his first thought was that, finally, after thirty years, a break must have come in the investigation of his sister's murder. Despite what may have been disappointment at talking to a newspaper reporter, he answered a few questions and then referred me to his sister Helen in Dalton. She, obviously pleased that somebody in Watertown still remembered, was most gracious and helpful.

I had hoped that Larry Cole, who had aspired to write a book about the Izak case, would work with me on the anniversary story, but a massive heart attack on March 27, 1998, claimed my would-be partner's life.

On June 10, 1998, the *Watertown Times* carried part one of my report, a recap about the unsolved murder on Wellesley Island. The second part appeared the following day, making public for the first time police questions about the activities of one of their colleagues, David Hennigan, on the night of the murder.

I quoted Polett talking about how his interview of Hennigan at Oneida was interrupted by the sudden arrival of the trooper's wife, Beverly, and about "certain things" in the trooper's account "that we were not satisfied with."

Polett, I reported, "suggested the trooper went too far in checking for life."

> *He was highly trained in first aid, more so than the average trooper. He rolled her over and up against himself to check for life, when all he had to do was go for a pulse and her carotid artery. Why handle the body to that extent?*

That second-day story coincided with Lisa's receipt of the state police denial of her Freedom of Information request.

Her inquiries on the Internet brought two responses. One came from Tacoma, Washington. Edward Fischer, a private detective with SRI Investigative Group, offered Lisa some suggestions, including one that she should contact me to obtain copies of all the *Watertown Times* stories about the murder. She tried calling me on June 16. Failing to reach me, she faxed a letter.

Lisa later told me she was nervous about contacting me. She would have been much more confident if only she had known how pleased I was to hear from her. The reporter's hopes were now bolstered. I had wondered whether anything would come from my journalistic effort. Might I have awakened a sleeping giant in Albany? Perhaps not, but somebody in the Izak family was ready to take on the giant.

I reached Lisa at her sister's home. During our telephone chat, I told her of the various sources who had expressed suspicion about the man who had reported Irene's murder.

"My heart started beating so fast," she told me. "A light bulb went on over my head that this was why the New York State Police wouldn't give me any information at all."

I told her I would help her in any way possible. I'm not sure I realized at that moment that this woman meant business and that she had every intention of taking advantage of my offer.

The second response to her Internet search came from another PI, this one closer to home. Augustine Papay of Port Jervis, New York, convinced Lisa that he, not somebody from out west in Tacoma, would be better suited to take on the case. He met with family members on July 4 in the Ewasko home in Dalton.

"I remember I didn't trust him at first, but I did when we met him in person at my parents' house that summer," Lisa said. "I finally had hope that something would be done, and maybe an arrest would be made."

The detective made an agreement with the family. He was taking on the case without a fee. His payback, he expected, would come in a wrongful death lawsuit in federal court.

A few days after his visit with the Izak family, Gus Papay telephoned me at the *Times*. He was coming to Watertown and asked to meet me. We rendezvoused in mid-July 1998 at a McDonald's near the east edge of Watertown. Gus was accompanied by his wife, Elizabeth.

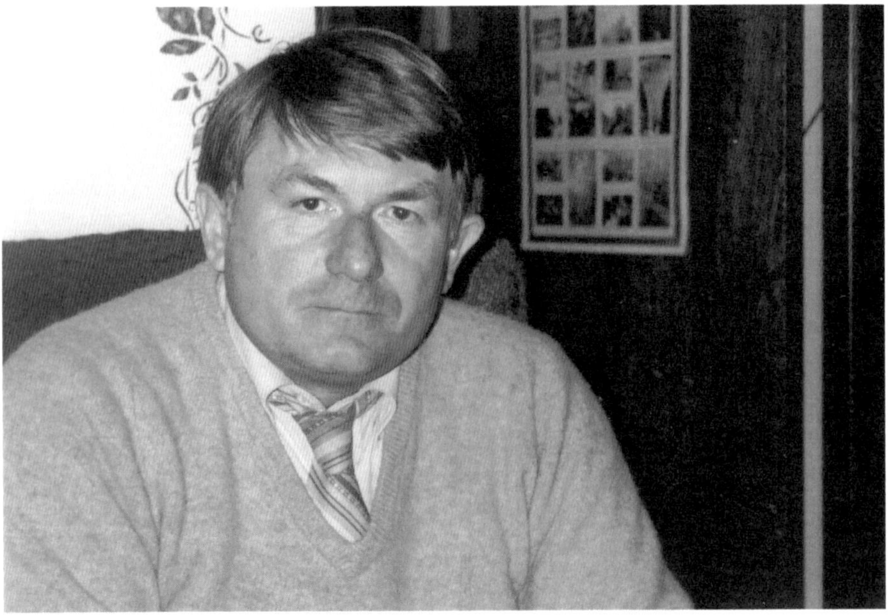

Gus Papay. *Photo by author.*

The paunchy, sandy-haired, retired New York City Housing Authority cop spoke in an accent that reflected a European background. Intent on convincing me of his qualifications, he pulled from an attaché his resume, outlining a career beginning in 1973 with the Housing Authority Police. He had patrolled in Manhattan, the Bronx and Queens until 1980, when he was transferred to the authority's internal affairs bureau. His initial responsibility had been background investigations on police officer job applicants, but eventually he was assigned to investigate criminal allegations against his fellow cops. Eventual promotions to detective and senior investigator placed him, in 1990, in the housing authority's detective bureau, working in violent street crime and homicide investigations.

From the attaché also came a couple of impressive press clippings.

A *New York* magazine feature that appeared on October 19, 1992, included a cover photo of Papay and New York City homicide detective Irwin "Silki" Silverman. The story "Portrait of a Serial Killer," by Stephen J. Dubner, summarized an investigation into the murder of Jessica Guzman two years earlier in the Bronx. The work of the two detectives resulted in the arrest and eventual conviction of Alejandro "Alex" Henriquez for three murders.

The two detectives had come together because in all homicides and major cases, the city police and housing authority officers work jointly. Papay was temporarily assigned to the Forty-third Precinct Homicide Task Force, partnered with Silverman.

The Guzman case was also the subject of a made-for-television movie that aired on the CBS television network.

Years later, after Papay had failed to endear himself to New York State Police in the Irene Izak homicide investigation, a couple of investigators, one retired and one still active, suggested to me that Papay had ridden on Silverman's coattails in the Guzman case. I eventually met Silverman and addressed that allegation to him. If anything, Silverman assured me, it was he, Silverman, who had ridden Papay's coattails.

Papay's feelings toward state troopers were quite mutual, probably dating back to when he was still an internal affairs investigator. Having left work late one night, he was making the hour-long drive to his home in Orange County when a trooper pulled him over.

The episode was described in "The Real Cop Land" by Glenn Thrush, which appeared in the August 18, 1997, issue of *New York* magazine.

"Shit," he remembers thinking. "It's two o'clock. I've got tinted windows. They think I'm carrying drugs."

After pulling over, Papay hung his shield and police ID out the window, as he'd done a dozen times before. Usually that did the trick, but this trooper wasn't inclined to extend professional courtesies.

"He tells me I was weaving on the road, which was total bullshit," says Papay, who retired from the force in 1994. "I tell him, 'I understand that you were profiling me. Don't lie to me—one cop to another.'"

The trooper, Papay says, told him to fuck off and started writing a summons. Papay exploded, scrambling out of the car. The upstater placed his hand on his gun. "And I'm almost reaching for mine, too," says Papay.

For a few moments, the men faced each other, teetering on the edge of cop-shoots-cop tabloid superstardom. "It could have turned into a fucking gun battle," Papay says.

"Easy."

But then he climbed back in his car and called 911. A supervisor shortly arrived and calmed the pair down. Papay was sent on his way without a summons.

Like the family he was representing, Papay was a refugee of an Iron Curtain nation, Hungary.

"After learning of their fierce flight from the Ukraine to the U.S. in seeking political freedom, I knew exactly what they went through to get here," Papay told me. "You could say that my similar European background contributed a cause for empathy for the Izak family."

When Papay was six, in 1956, his divorced father fled his homeland. The Communist government harassed and persecuted small-business owners, withholding materials from them to force them out of business, Papay said. His father, owner of a sheet metal shop, took advantage of an uprising by his countrymen to escape Hungary, going to Austria. Augustine Papay Sr. subsequently moved to the United States, finding a factory job in Syracuse, New York.

The father and son were reunited in November 1963 after the young Papay was granted a passport by the Hungarian government to live with his father, who by then had settled in New York City, where he was working for a sheet metal roofing company.

The junior Papay accompanied his godparents on a train to Vienna, Austria. There, he was greeted by his father, and the pair boarded a train for Koblenz, West Germany. Then came another railway transfer, this time to take them to Luxembourg. As they changed trains, a fellow passenger noticed that the elder Papay had an English magazine in his hand and asked if he was American. That affirmed, the stranger, speaking in broken English, asked Mr. Papay if he had heard the news from the United States.

"Your president, John F. Kennedy, was just assassinated," the man said.

"I didn't understand the conversation," Papay said, "but I could tell that my father's expression became like if he was in a state of shock."

Gus asked what the man had said.

"My father turned to me with teary eyes and said, 'They killed President Kennedy.'"

With the sun's rising on November 24, the thirteen-year-old lad peered out his window, viewing beautiful scenery and one ruined castle after another as the train rattled its way along the winding banks of the Rhine River. At Luxembourg, father and son said goodbye to Europe, flying to New York City. Their trip across the Atlantic brought them to New York International Airport, destined to be renamed JFK.

The teenager's eyes became fixed on two uniformed cops who were on duty in the international arrivals building.

"To me it was like a natural attraction, not only to the uniform, but also to the profession itself, because ever since my childhood I knew that I wanted to become a police officer. I also knew that it was just a matter of time before I would be wearing the same uniform with the shiny badge and gun."

Papay and I sat in McDonald's for more than an hour discussing the Izak case. He reviewed my *Times* articles and asked for my suggestions about potential interviews. Blessed with a typical North Country sunny July afternoon, we then drove the thirty-some miles up Interstate 81 to the Thousand Islands Bridge. At the tollbooth, Papay asked the collector about the layout here thirty years ago. The man in the booth was unsure.

A few minutes later, we were on Wellesley Island. I directed my new acquaintance to take the first exit and then turn left onto Jefferson County Route 91, the former Route 81 extension that had led Irene Izak on the road to her death.

The interstate's four-lane run to the next bridge, the span crossing an arm of the St. Lawrence River to Canada's Hill Island, had been completed two years after the murder. No longer was a steady flow of traffic passing by the rest area and ditch where the young woman was robbed of her life.

As we proceeded up the old highway, Papay pointed out a couple of locations where he guessed somebody, possibly a cop in an unmarked car, might have parked and waited for an unsuspecting motorist to approach. After we parked in the same rest area where Irene had stopped thirty years earlier, Papay carefully worked his way down into the ditch to get a feel for the crime scene. He would later return here with Polett's former partner, Charles Donoghue, to get a clearer picture of where Irene had died.

Finally, on that night of our acquaintance, Papay placed in my hand the watch that Irene had worn the day of her murder. I felt a chill rush through my body and quickly returned it to him.

Papay drove to Pennsylvania to interview Ray Polett. He pressed me to track down people who might have worked with and associated with David Hennigan, although he asserted that we should never isolate ourselves to one suspect. Despite that warning, he focused on Hennigan and spent some time tailing him to learn his routines. He attended Mass at Our Lady of the Sacred Heart Church and filmed Hennigan in his role as deacon.

One of Hennigan's former colleagues in the state police suggested that Papay look into another death investigation simply because of one coincidence: while Hennigan was active in the Boy Scouts, the victim had died near a Girl Scout camp, which neighbored a similar facility for boys.

Alissa Lynn Audo, ten, had disappeared early on the morning of July 28, 1963, from her tent at Camp Trefoil in the Adirondacks in southern St. Lawrence County. Her partially clothed body was found a day later in a heavily wooded section a mile away from the camp. Some bruises were found on her body, but nothing to prove assault, and she had not been sexually molested, police said. Authorities did not elaborate on her cause of death, other than to specify lung congestion. Of particular note was the girl's tendency toward sleepwalking.

If she was indeed murdered, state police identified a suspect, a young man who lived in the area. The only similarity Papay found in the two cases was the inability of state police to develop evidence to support a murder charge.

During his review of the Izak investigation, Papay drew on the expertise of two former associates at the New York Police Department, Silki Silverman and Raymond Pierce, who had specialized as a psychological profiler. Among their suggestions was a manner in which one or more members of the Izak family might confront Hennigan, perhaps after a Mass at Sacred Heart Church. Such an event never occurred, in deference to a revived state police investigation.

After reporting back to the family about his activities, Papay wrote a four-page letter, dated September 18, 1998, and signed by Helen and Paul Ewasko, that he mailed to New York governor George E. Pataki, asking for his intervention. The document brought up ten issues:

1. The discrepancies between Irene's speed on Interstate 81 alleged by Hennigan and the speed capability of her Volkswagen, as determined by Polett and Donoghue.
2. Hennigan, as the man who found the body, had failed to offer condolences to the family.
3. Hennigan had given to his state police colleagues varying versions of how he got Irene's blood on his uniform.
4. Hennigan allegedly had a history of domestic violence and violent rage attacks.
5. Hennigan was attracted to pornographic materials.
6. Hennigan's official statement and alibi were never satisfactory.
7. Hennigan's uniform raincoat, which he likely wore on the night of the murder, disappeared.
8. Hennigan regularly asked his supervising officer for use of an unmarked car.
9. Irene "expressed an emotion of fear" about Hennigan when she spoke to the toll collector at the Thousand Islands Bridge.
10. A man who was called "the Heathen" by his state police colleagues eventually became religious after the murder and became an ordained Catholic Church deacon.

They asked that all old evidence be submitted to a forensic laboratory for application of the latest developments in police science, including serology and DNA testing, and that the bloodstained state trooper's uniform be inspected by a blood-spatter expert. Also requested was the appointment of a state police liaison to work with Papay in the investigation.

Although asserting that they were not accusing state police of having exercised a cover-up, the Ewasko letter asserted:

> *We have trusted the State Police all this time and we were content that as professional law enforcement officers they would deal with this case as professionals should. However, with all due respect to their service, their profession and their dedication, we as reasonable common folks cannot*

willfully ignore the ten elements of facts noted above, and therefore we have serious questions to raise with the New York State Police.

We know that the Division of New York State Police is a semi military style police force whose ranking commanders are very concerned about the image of the members of their Department. We sincerely hope that the Troop D Division commanders from 1968 to 1998 were not trying to protect their untouchable image of their members, whereby they also may have blindly and unwillingly protected the murderer of our sister.

INVESTIGATION TO NOWHERE, PART II

The voice on the phone identified himself to Helen Ewasko as Captain John E. Wood, with the New York State Police Bureau of Criminal Investigation at Oneida. This was the call that she had been anticipating.

The letter to the New York governor, prepared by Gus Papay and adjusted and signed by Paul and Helen Ewasko, had produced results—and quickly.

"He said Governor Pataki had told them to reinvestigate Irene's murder," Helen said. "I couldn't believe it was happening. It was a good feeling, knowing that something was being done."

Captain Wood requested and was granted a meeting with family members. He would not be disappointed by the family turnout a few days later. As Senior Investigator Richard H. Ladue from the Watertown headquarters; Senior Investigator Stanley E. Weidman, assigned to the violent crimes unit at Oneida; and his supervisor, Lieutenant Thomas P. Connelly, entered the Ewasko home at Dalton, Pennsylvania, on Tuesday, October 20, 1998, they found sixteen family members ready to hear them out. Paul and Helen were joined by their daughter, Lisa Caputo. Stephen and Luba Boyko had come down from Conklin, New York, and from the Philadelphia suburb of Warminster came Zenon George, his wife, Christine, and their son, John. The youngest of the Izak siblings, Nicholas, was present, but the oldest, Andrew, in poor health, could not attend. Representing him was his daughter, Daria McDonnell.

And Gus Papay was there.

"I felt that they were not comfortable with Gus being there," Daria said. "It seemed that whenever he had a comment or the family asked a question regarding anything that Gus had suspected or found, they were not forthright with us."

The family initially found their official visitors appearing to be nervous. "I think they thought we were going to be hostile," said Lisa, who described herself as "excited, nervous and so hopeful" at this meeting. "Once they realized that we weren't hostile, they relaxed," she said.

The investigators opened by apologizing that the family had not been kept informed over the years about what was being done in the case. They also quickly emphasized that this discussion should be considered highly confidential because they didn't want "him" to become aware of a "very active investigation," Daria said.

The captive audience heard the investigators discuss how Trooper Hennigan had told different versions of how he had gotten Irene's blood on his uniform and had used the phrase "ass end over teacup" in one of his explanations. They were also told about the day when Beverly Hennigan had interrupted the interrogation session in Oneida, leading her husband out of the interview room—"a legal right, from what we were told," Daria said.

She said she saw pain in the face of Steve Boyko as he recalled for the investigators the day he had gone to Watertown to identify the body of his slain sister-in-law. Her aunt Helen had never heard Steve talk about the experience, she said.

"I remember thinking how sad it was that he kept this to himself to protect those he loved," Daria said.

Luba and Helen opened an album to give the investigators a glimpse into Irene's life and shared stories about her. And the two women insisted that their sister would not have voluntarily stopped for anybody on a roadside. She had promised.

"We are making her an actual person instead of just a statistic," Daria observed. "They did listen and I believe took it to heart."

Then came a question that the family had likely not expected. The state police sought permission to exhume Irene's body.

"This is unreal," Daria thought to herself. "My heart started beating real fast. I was almost in disbelief, but at the same time very excited that this could be the one thing that would resolve this, and finally our families would find some closure."

Her thoughts turned to her father, the one sibling who could not attend. This should be kept from him, she believed, because of his poor health.

"I also thought about my grandparents, wondering if they would be upset with us for doing this. How would they feel about us disturbing Irene's final resting place?"

What were the others thinking, she wondered.

There was silence.

"Imagining disturbing Irene in her grave, it was a profoundly painful decision," Paul Ewasko said.

Luba and Helen looked at each other, as if in a mutual plea for guidance. George and Nicholas sat stoically. George "was obviously having a very hard time dealing internally with the question," Paul said.

Paul offered his opinion that if an exhumation could help develop evidence that might make the difference in bringing justice for Irene, it was worth a try. Steve Boyko concurred. One by one, the four siblings reluctantly signed consent forms.

As the investigative team left the Ewasko home, it warned family members against building up expectations, "but I think we all had high hopes that day," Daria said.

A month passed and winter was arriving, but no exhumation was scheduled. Paul Ewasko telephoned Jefferson County's district attorney, James T. King, asking about the delay. There was a question of who would pay the approximately $5,000 in costs, New York State or Jefferson County, he was told. More calls were made, with state police division headquarters ultimately informing the Oneida command that state police would bear the cost.

That resolved, King filed a request for authorization of an exhumation "for such physical, chemical or other examination or analysis as they [state police] may deem appropriate, with cost to be borne by the New York State Police." On December 10, 1998, the exhumation order was issued by state Supreme Court justice Hugh A. Gilbert in Watertown.

Finally, on the morning of December 30—thirty years and six months after the burial of Irene Izak—a digging crew, New York State Police, family and friends gathered at St. Vladimir's Cemetery for the exhumation. The family was kept at a distance, most seeking the warmth of the cemetery's chapel. But they stole glimpses of the project, quietly observing as a coffin was unearthed and placed into a hearse.

There had been water damage to the coffin, they were told, but skeletal remains were available for examination by Dr. Michael Baden and his forensic pathology team.

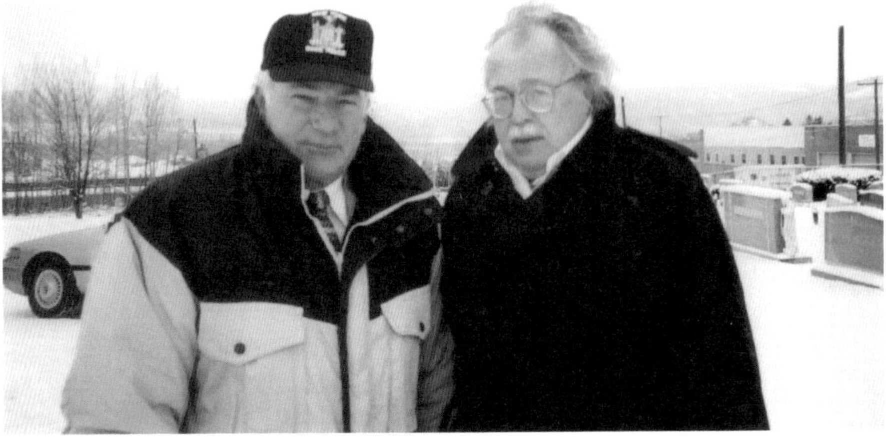

Lieutenant Thomas P. Connelly, New York State Police, and Dr. Michael Baden await Irene's exhumation at St. Vladimir's Cemetery, Scranton, Pennsylvania. *Photo by author.*

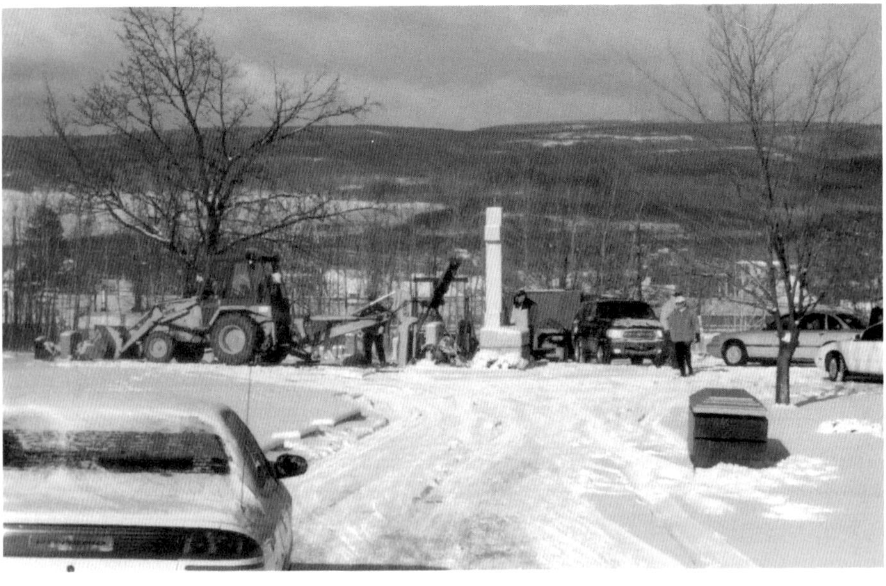

The exhumation begins. *Photo by author.*

Dr. Baden, the state police pathologist, came with a national reputation in his field. In 1977, he had been given charge of a congressional select committee on assassinations for reexamination of the autopsy conducted on assassinated president John F. Kennedy. His team of scientists

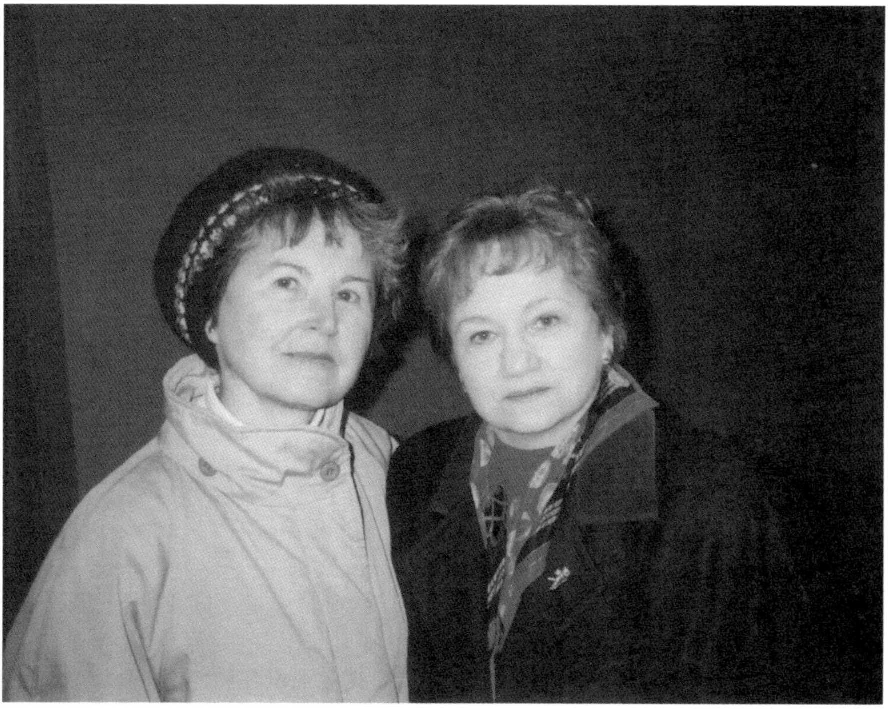

Luba Boyko and Helen Ewasko wait on December 30, 1998, for the exhumation of their slain sister's remains. *Photo by author.*

concluded the November 1963 autopsy was a "forensic disaster." More recently, in 1995, he had served as a defense witness during a nine-month trial of former National Football League star O.J. Simpson, accused of murdering his estranged wife, Nicole, and Ronald Goldman at her home in California.

Accompanying Dr. Baden in this Scranton investigation was Dr. Lowell J. Levine, a forensic scientist and doctor of dental surgery who brought equally impressive credentials. He had served as a consultant to the 1977 JFK select committee team and had testified at serial killer Ted Bundy's trial. Dr. Levine was among American forensic scientists who, in 1992–93, participated in an effort to confirm identities of skeletal remains from a mass grave as those of the family of Russian tsar Nicholas II.

After conducting their preliminary examination on Irene's skeleton at Moses Taylor Hospital, Scranton, the state police team met that afternoon with the family and Gus Papay in a hospital conference room.

Investigators asked that the reporter be excluded. I understood my place, and it was not in that room.

Irene's skull, found in multiple pieces, was in need of repair to continue the forensic investigation, Dr. Baden told the family. With their permission, the skull would be sent to Florida for reconstruction. State police did not specify where, but Papay said such work in Florida is conducted at the Forensic Anthropology Department at the University of Gainesville, which had a working relationship with New York State Police.

The family consented, again after an emotional conversation.

A committal service was held in the evening, with the coffin containing partial remains being placed alongside the resting places of Irene's parents, Bohdan and Maria.

Less than two months later, on February 17, 1999, Helen Ewasko was informed by Lieutenant Connelly that "interesting" results had been derived from the autopsy.

Dr. Anthony B. Falsetti, director of the University of Gainesville facility, declined to tell me how long his staff of graduate students had worked on the skull or to discuss findings. He generalized that each case takes between two and four weeks. Each bone or fragment would have been laid out in anatomical position and assigned an identifying number. The team routinely examines the remains for both disease and trauma, he said, and records findings with photographs and radiographs.

Irene's skull was not returned to its resting place until May 2002.

Meanwhile, I waited impatiently to do my job. Respecting the state police's request for secrecy, the *Watertown Daily Times* agreed not to report that an exhumation had been conducted and that the investigation into the murder of Irene Izak had been revived.

My competitive journalist's nature left me concerned that the Scranton news media might learn of the event at their nearby cemetery and would break the news. That did not happen.

As state police investigators reinterviewed people who were involved in the probe three decades earlier, talk soon circulated in Watertown that something was moving in the Izak case. Again, I was nervous. Would the competing media in Watertown expose the story I was sitting on?

I had nothing to worry about. Not only did they not break the story, but also, to our great disappointment, Watertown's two television stations ignored the story after I was able to report new developments in the case. Only one radio newsman paid attention.

As the investigation progressed, a portion of the uniform worn by David Hennigan on the night of the murder was submitted to a laboratory for blood-splatter analysis. The problem here, my sources told me, was that perhaps there was not a sufficient amount of the uniform remaining to provide an adequate examination.

Other laboratory examinations, not defined by state police, were also apparently conducted. DNA evidence was not a factor, I was told. After all, there was no question about whose blood was on the uniform. Whether any DNA was extracted from Irene's remains that might point to a murder suspect is a question state police would not answer.

Investigators refused to confirm to me that they were focused on one suspect, but in their reports to the family, their comments regarded one man, the retired state trooper. In the meantime, the family, Papay and I were waiting for the day to come when an attempt would be made to interview David Hennigan. Although state police never confirmed it to me, that day finally came in mid-June.

"People are up here doing things as we speak and should be taking him in for questioning soon," one of my sources, a retired investigator, told me in a telephone conversation on June 15, 1999. "I can't imagine him doing anything other than saying 'screw you,'" the source continued. "They are getting their ducks in a row, learning his habits. The time and place are vital, and they have to get him away from his wife."

Information later given to me, not by state police, was that investigators halted Hennigan's car on Interstate 81 near Watertown. They invited him to come along with them for an interview, to a motel room they had rented as a neutral place for the session. The former state trooper refused to join them.

The attempt to intercept Hennigan was confirmed in the letter written by Father Freeh to Steve Boyko:

> *This may sound like the movies, but they came upon him with an unmarked car and two patrol cars, all told seven cops, like he was some kind of "desparado." David told me—and I have no reason to doubt him—that they wanted him to go to a motel and talk. All I would see in this is an attempt to shake him up, not an attempt to engage him in purposeful dialogue.*

In the same letter, Father Freeh expressed another view about Hennigan's bloodstained uniform:

I was told by one of his fellow officers that there was no "splattered" blood on his uniform, only soaked blood, consistent with his impulsive act to elevate the head of the victim as a corpsman would likely do. I can say, from my knowledge of David, that his background in nursing would have likely prevailed over his training as a policeman.

My story about the exhumation and investigation broke on August 8, 1999. "We have not established enough evidence to establish culpability to substantiate an arrest or to complete successful prosecution," said Weidman in the story. Of the exhumation, he said that "further extensive forensics investigations have provided new and additional information."

What he did not disclose publicly was that the examination revealed Irene was most likely killed by a single blow with a weapon to the back of her head. The rage with which her killer had so viciously pummeled her head with rocks had been unnecessary. His mission had been accomplished with one swing of his arm.

A search for a facsimile of the suspected murder weapon—a flashlight—was attempted. I was never given a definite answer about the success of that effort.

Investigators interviewed "numerous" people, Weidman said, but "only one has declined to be interviewed and has sought the advice of counsel." He left for conjecture the name of that person.

Through my own inquiries, I determined that state police did not contact three women who were acquaintances of Irene, nor did they approach David Fleming, the first trooper other than Hennigan to arrive at the murder scene. They explained that Fleming was not consulted because he was left with impaired memory by a serious auto accident—which I had indeed found when I visited him—and besides, the written statement he had provided in 1968 was still in the evidence file.

Also in the file was the statement given by the bridge toll collector who had a brief visit with Irene. The document is inadmissible as evidence in a state court, however, because Clifford Putnam, the collector, is not alive to vouch for its accuracy.

Among the three women whom I had located, with Papay's assistance, was Maxine Postle, who had received a phone call from Irene that fateful night. After I told a state police deputy superintendent in Albany where the women could be found, investigators talked with at least two of them.

The offerings of these women might have done little to assist in the investigation, but still, the fact that investigators had not tracked them down left a question in my mind about how in-depth a probe was being conducted. Papay had offered his assistance to state police, but he was kept on the outside. The explanation given to me by an investigator was that state police rarely use the assistance of outsiders, particularly private detectives.

Soon after the investigation was revived, division headquarters notified Papay that Captain Wood was to be his liaison, but the captain never contacted him or returned his calls. Investigator Weidman spoke to Papay on a few occasions—when Gus called.

In the meantime, I heard a fair share of criticism being directed by state police at Papay. A retired investigator echoed what current members were alleging: "He's not careful. He is using innuendo and rumor and turning them into facts."

Papay was convinced that state police had bungled their attempt to interview Hennigan. Following the recommendation of one of his consultants, retired New York City police psychologist Raymond Pierce, Papay had suggested to state police that the best timing for approaching Hennigan would be at Sacred Heart Church, after he had assisted at Mass.

The private detective brought his case to the United States attorney in Syracuse, Daniel J. French. He hoped the federal government would be able to prosecute a charge that Irene's civil rights had been violated and would be able to use some of the evidence restricted from New York courts, such as the Putnam statement. French expressed an interest in the case, conferred with state police and offered his office's assistance wherever possible. But he came to a determination that the private detective did not expect.

Following a consultation with French, Papay brought disappointing news to the family in September. In 1968, there was a ten-year statute of limitations for prosecuting a charge of violating a person's civil rights. A death penalty phrase had been enacted in 1992 for such a crime, eliminating the statute of limitations, but the old law still applied for an incident in 1968.

"I feel the system is letting us down, and a murderer is laughing in our face," an angry and disappointed Gus Papay said.

French's comment to me was: "We are unaware of a statute that would allow us to actively prosecute the case, but if that changes and we find any way we can participate, we will."

Gus Papay also made a contact to stir some media attention in New York City about the cold case in northern New York. Mary Murphy, with WB11-TV, drove to Jefferson County with Papay and filmed a report that would be shown in two segments, on August 18 and the following night. One of her stops was near Dexter, a village west of Watertown, to a home off the shore of Lake Ontario.

In an unexpected interruption at his front door, the ashen-haired retired cop David Hennigan was staring at a television reporter and her cameraman, camera in hand. He was again being asked about the woman whose blood had stained his uniform thirty-one years earlier.

His face expressionless, Hennigan offered repeated no comments. But Mary Murphy, who had Papay waiting nearby in a car, was not about to leave without an answer.

"But you had nothing to do with Miss Izak's death?" Murphy persisted.

Shaking his head slowly, and closing his eyes, Hennigan answered, "I was working that night. I had nothing to do with her death."

He then referred the reporter to his lawyer, not providing a name, and offered one more quick comment: "I didn't have any rights then. I do now."

Although no other statements were made by Hennigan, Father Freeh spoke out in a letter that appeared on September 16, 1999, in the *Watertown Daily Times*.

"While I can in some way understand the rush to judgment that so characterized and flawed the investigation at the onset," he wrote, "I cannot even begin to comprehend how a reporter like Mr. Shampine could perpetuate that grievous error and add to the calumny that ignorant people have already circulated in regard to Mr. Hennigan."

He alleged that Hennigan was questioned without the presence of a lawyer, "under extremely adversarial conditions for a full day and an entire night immediately after the incident." Of the two lie detector tests, he said Hennigan "was never officially told the results."

In the first test, which was inconclusive, "they didn't get what they wanted," and the second "clearly showed he was telling the truth," the priest wrote.

Polett denied that the questioning of Hennigan on June 10, 1968, lasted as long as alleged in the priest's letter, but he acknowledged, "It would not be unusual to question any murder suspect several hours…Who else would you question more at length? Hennigan was at the scene, and he had been with the victim earlier that night."

Father Freeh alleged that police failed to follow certain leads, including a witness's report that two men were seen near Irene's car, and "a man who had been in the area was later found dead of suicide with bloody clothes in his car."

I asked investigators about this reported suicide. One seemed puzzled, unaware of any such connection, while the official response in Albany was the standard "no comment" that I was given for the majority of my questions.

Father Freeh said I had failed to report that Hennigan "was reinstated as a Police officer." Reinstatement did not happen, my police sources told me, because he was never suspended.

"I am indebted to Mr. Shampine for one thing," the priest continued. "He has made public the fact that, far from trying to orchestrate a coverup, BCI Investigator Ray Polett and his associates were trying to pin the murder on a trooper they wanted to make out as a rogue cop."

On December 1, 1999, family members met in Albany with state police superintendent James W. McMahon, and at their disposal for their questions were eighteen people who were involved in the investigation, including Cindy F. Intschert, who had succeeded Jim King as Jefferson County district attorney. A representative from French's office was also present. Drs. Baden and Levine were there, along with another member of their staff, Dr. Barbara Wolf.

"They all seemed very up-front," Lisa Caputo said. "They answered any questions that we had in as much detail as they were allowed."

The six family members who came were introduced to the retired Ray Rasmussen, a man who had been targeted by Papay with harsh criticism for a botched investigation in 1968. Papay had characterized Rasmussen as a man so ambitious to climb in the ranks of state police that he would not want to be "embarrassed" by one of his troopers being a murder suspect. Papay's opinion was fueled by hindsight, since Rasmussen did indeed advance through the ranks, becoming in 1983 the second man in the chain of command as first deputy superintendent.

"We were touched by the fact that he never forgot about my aunt's case and to see how emotional he was when he spoke about it," Lisa said.

He seemed to "choke up" as he spoke about Irene's unsolved murder, Paul Ewasko recalled. "Just before we departed, Rasmussen shook Helen's hand and said he was very sorry about Irene. He looked sad and said he felt badly for our family since he, too, wanted Irene's murder solved."

Lisa said she left the session feeling confident that state police were doing everything they could in the investigation. As family spokesperson that night, she told me, "We were highly impressed by the intensity of the investigation and are optimistic that the case will be solved."

Some forensic tests were still being conducted by the FBI, she said. I sought comments from Superintendent McMahon and was given a brief statement by the state police public affairs office. He said in the release, "I place great importance on working closely with the families…of violent and senseless acts…State police will leave no stone unturned in trying to bring responsible parties to justice, no matter how long it takes."

I asked an investigator why District Attorney Intschert did not present the circumstantial evidence to a grand jury to seek a sealed indictment. The answer given me was that a case can be presented only once, so if a "no-bill" or refusal to indict were returned, the case could not again be presented, even if new evidence were developed.

Papay's reaction was that he had seen weaker cases prosecuted, and at this stage, more than three decades after the killing, he felt there was nothing to lose by letting a grand jury hear the evidence.

Lisa and her uncle Steve decided to make a direct approach to Hennigan. Both wrote to him, with Lisa asking him to help her understand what happened to her aunt that night. Steve's letter was more direct and challenging to Hennigan. Neither letter was answered.

Steve Boyko wrote to Hennigan's bishop, Gerald M. Barbarito, in Ogdensburg, New York, asking for his intervention. He said, in part:

> *I pray Deacon David will help us alleviate some of the pain the family feels, even more so today. I, Stephen, for the family of Irene, am asking you to talk with Deacon David, ask him to present himself and talk with the investigators, help bring relief to a family who still mourns for Irene.*

Bishop Barbarito offered his sympathy, understanding and prayers in a letter dated August 9, 2000, but abstained from assisting:

> *At the same time, as far as David Hennigan's participation is concerned, he has exercised his right before the laws of New York State and our country to obtain legal counsel. His attorney is the one responsible for guiding his response at the present time. Before our judicial system, he has the right to*

> *decline further comment on the matter in any public forum, without prejudice or implication in terms of personal responsibility for the original tragic event. I must be respectful of his rights as a citizen as far as that is concerned.*

There were more meetings between family and investigators, prompted by Steve Boyko's determination that the prior thirty years of silence would not be resumed. But Paul, Helen, Steve and Luba were forced to face reality in a discussion on October 5, 2004, at Oneida.

"We were told that everything that could be done has been done," Paul told me.

> *All kinds of suppositions exist that can point to Hennigan, but without physical evidence he still walks free. They assured us that Irene's case continues to be reviewed. They are frustrated that the law prevents them from interrogating or even approaching him.*

I drove to Albany and met with a deputy superintendent of state police, seeking some answers about the police investigation. I left frustrated by unanswered questions, so I filed a request under the state's Freedom of Information Law for certain details. I asked for a copy of the initial crime report, handwritten notations made in the Watertown station's desk blotter on the morning of the murder and copies of reports relating to the interviews of two "Jane Doe" witnesses, purported to be waitresses. I also sought copies of the toll collector's statement, of an "unusual incident report" that may have been sent by Major Rasmussen to the state police superintendent, of any complaints and disciplines possibly involving the trooper and of reports relating to the investigative inspections of Irene's car and the trooper's car.

I knew I was really pushing when I also asked for information about the two polygraph examinations administered to Hennigan, but I saw no reason why state police should not grant my final request: specification of the location of a public telephone used by Irene two hours prior to her murder and confirmation of where her call was directed.

Without exception, my requests were declined on the grounds that "these are records which were compiled for law enforcement purposes and which, if disclosed, would interfere with a law enforcement investigation."

I brought my plight to Robert J. Freeman, executive director of the New York Committee on Open Government. In a ten-page "advisory opinion" issued on February 25, 2003, Freeman supported me in the majority of my requests, telling state police, "In view of the fact that nearly thirty-five years have passed since the murder, it is inconceivable that every aspect of every record relating to the murder would, if disclosed, interfere with an investigation."

He surprised me with a finding that I was entitled to information regarding possible complaints and disciplines involving the trooper. He wrote:

> *Insofar as records pertaining to the trooper reflect a determination indicating a finding of misconduct, an admission of misconduct or any penalty imposed as a result of such a finding or admission, I believe that they must be disclosed.*

Freeman's opinion was not binding upon state police, however. My renewed request under the Freedom of Information Law was again denied.

During the early stages of the state police–revived investigation, I had asked an investigator if they would consider consulting a psychic. What did they have to lose? But his reaction was one of disinterest, and the police, to my knowledge, never ventured onto that avenue.

Papay and I did, however. Separately.

A Jefferson County woman who had assisted police agencies in the past accompanied me to Wellesley Island on July 24, 2000. Penny E. Parish, who charged no fee, said she had not read my stories about the murder and had no knowledge about it.

We had not been standing long in the parking area overlooking the ditch where Irene was murdered when my companion began rambling. She said she was in contact with Irene. But Irene was not talking to her, she said. Parish said she was "seeing pictures."

"He was very friendly to her…when he pulled her over," the psychic said. "They did a lot of conversing. He told her to be careful at driving that late at night."

Parish said the man offered to take her to coffee. Suddenly, my companion's manner changed.

"My head is throbbing. Did he hit her in the head? It wasn't a billy club; it was leather, actually."

She described the object as being six to eight inches long. "Policemen carried them at the time. And they were leather."

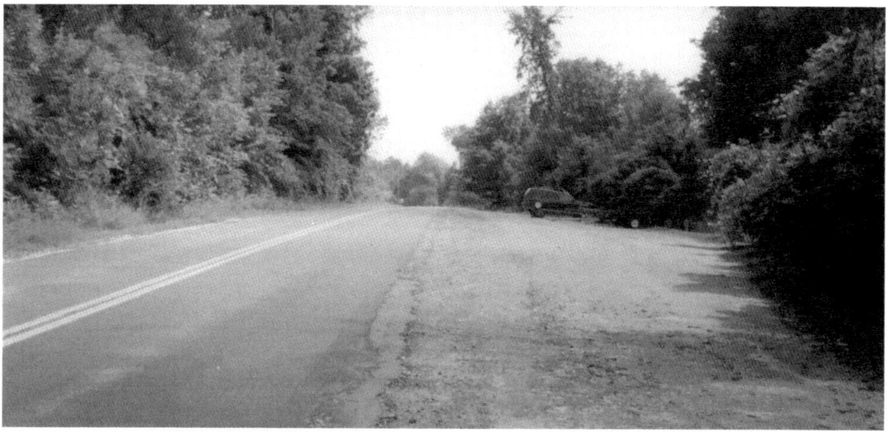

Decades later, the rest area where Irene Izak made her last stop is tranquil, the road having long been abandoned as the island's Interstate 81 extension. *Photo by author.*

Papay later told me she had described a blackjack, or a "slapper."

"I don't see him killing her here," Parish said, an obvious flaw in her account.

Minutes later, she said she saw Irene in the man's car, and then she saw the man giving Irene an ultimatum, demanding that she perform a sexual act with him. "She wouldn't do it," the psychic said. "He got angry."

During the summer of 2004, Papay met at Niagara Falls with a medium whom he said is listed among the top one hundred psychics in America, B. Anne Gehman of Lily Dale, New York. From his session, he reported that Gehman saw Irene rejecting a sexual approach, felt pain in the back of her head and felt some strangulation.

Paul Ewasko disclosed from a state police briefing that there was evidence of a slight attempt at strangulation.

Papay said Gehman also sensed that the killer had stalked Irene's car before reaching the rest area and had disposed of his raincoat in "moving water" near a bridge.

The killer enjoyed pornography, she said. She also had unexplained sightings of a vicious dog and a small man in religious life playing a violin, and she asked about somebody named Yatta or Etta. Those possible links are undetermined.

Parish, in her visit with me at the site, said that "some hair was missing." She later added, "Especially the hair in the back. It looked like it, I don't know, like her hair had been pulled."

Papay reported that Gehman said the killer took "small trophies," then she saw hair and asked if Irene's hair was pulled.

Both psychics believed that the man who killed Irene Izak had killed before.

"But she isn't the first one," Parish said. "She isn't the only one, I guess I should say. It would be interesting to know if even in Canada there is still a missing blonde."

In Niagara Falls, Papay said he was told of "possibly three others," including one perhaps in Tennessee and another along Interstate 81 somewhere south of Watertown.

I knew of no other similar murders "south of Watertown," but that vague suggestion could cover any number of miles.

When Papay agreed to investigate the case for the family, an option he anticipated was a wrongful death lawsuit in federal court demanding damages from New York State, state police, Jefferson County and David Hennigan. But with criminal prosecution not having developed, plans for a civil lawsuit languished until August 2004, when a criminal defense lawyer in Watertown contacted me. He told me that he had long been interested in the case, and he believed the family should act quickly to file civil action before all the involved principals are gone.

His motives were not for personal gain because he was suggesting that I refer the family to a lawyer in Albany. If there was anybody in the state who could find a loophole for a lawsuit, he said, his nominee in Albany was that person.

I relayed this message of a possible last hope to family members in Pennsylvania. There was hesitance and resistance on their part. They did not want to give an impression that they were seeking financial gain from Irene's death, and they also did not want to set themselves up for another disappointment after they had endured so many setbacks.

Ultimately, they agreed to this one final try, hoping that a lawsuit might force the state to try harder to reconcile the investigation of 1968. If any damages could be won, they vowed that all proceeds would be placed in a charity in memory of Irene.

Their letter to an Albany law office, in which they requested an appointment, brought them only another unanticipated wait. The attorney never acknowledged receiving their letter, and it was not until a few months later, in 2005, that he declined the case without comment.

In the decade that followed the renewed Izak investigation, I had passing meetings with David Hennigan. There were glancing moments on three occasions in a supermarket, where we had quick exchanges of "hello." He offered perhaps a split second of eye contact. Our paths crossed once in a bank and another time in a medical office. Never was a second word expressed by either of us.

We did, however, have a mail exchange. I wrote to Hennigan in August 2004, making my second written request for an interview. His reply alleged that my newspaper stories about the murder "consisted of a great deal of your personal theory, innuendo, and speculation along with theory and speculation of your sources, which have no foundation in fact or truth."

A couple paragraphs later, he added:

> *Perhaps I judge you harshly; perhaps you are not a "yellow" journalist; perhaps you're not the same person as described by some of your colleagues in the news media, local law enforcement personnel, and individuals your journalism has hurt over the years. Perhaps you should consider the effect*

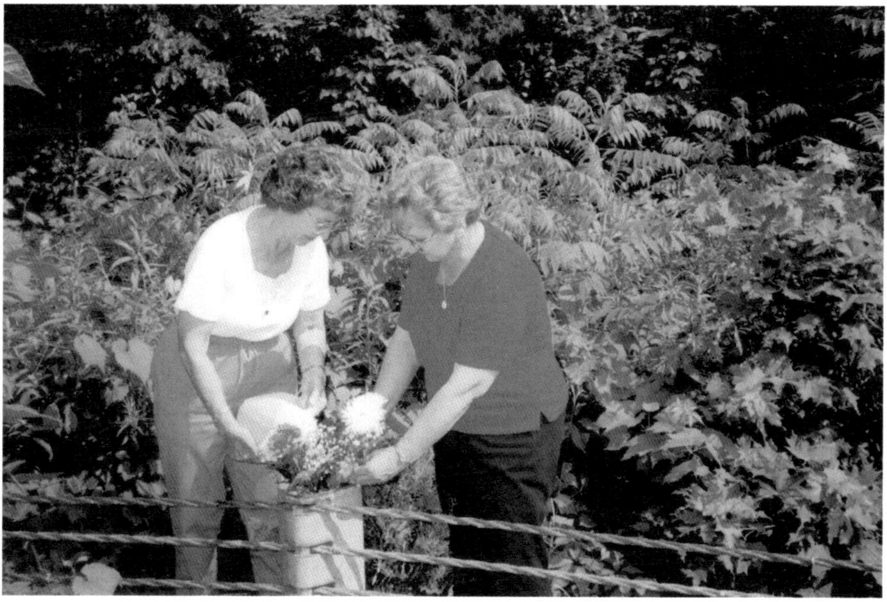

Luba Boyko and Helen Ewasko placed flowers at the site of their sister's murder during an emotional visit about three decades after the murder. *Photo by author.*

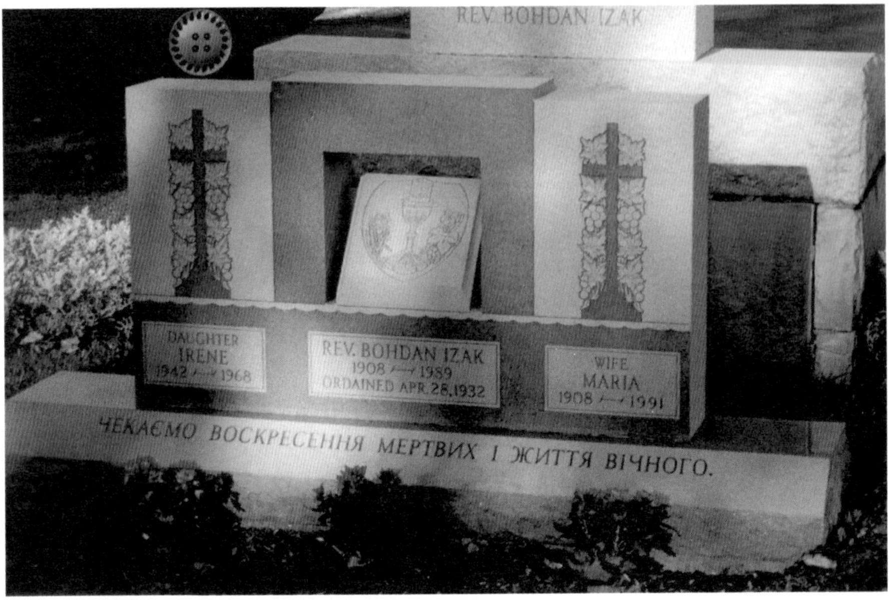

Irene's final resting place is with her parents, Bohdan and Maria. *Photo by author.*

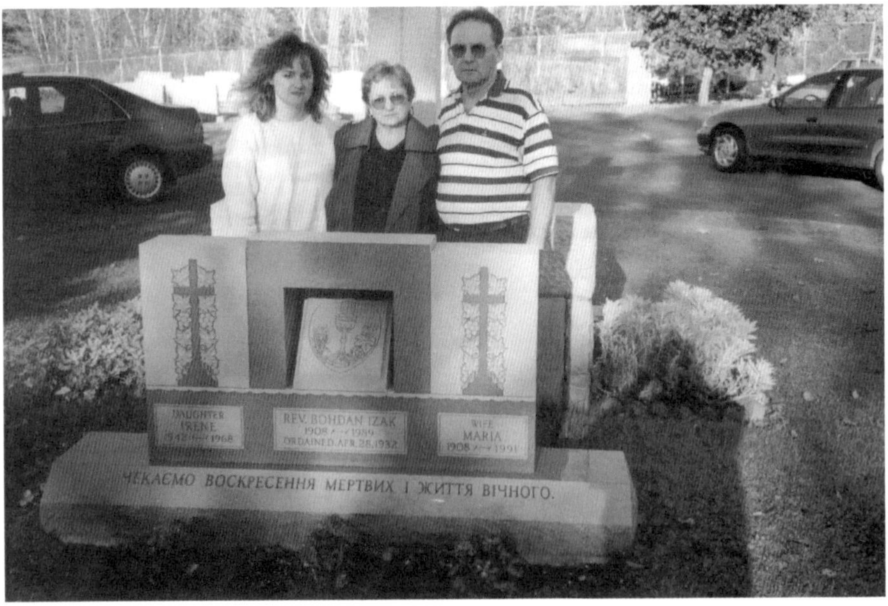

Lisa Caputo (left) and her parents, Helen and Paul Ewasko, visit Irene's grave. *Photo by author.*

> *that your journalism has on individuals and their families and report the facts not embellish them with your or others personal agendas.*

He closed with a warning: "I suggest you take into consideration the laws regarding libel, defamation and slander as you proceed."

On March 3, 2009, six days after he had assisted at Sacred Heart Church's Ash Wednesday observance, at about 2:50 p.m., as I worked at my desk at the *Watertown Daily Times*, I heard on the police scanner an ambulance dispatch to the Hennigan residence near Dexter. The initial report was that a seventy-year-old man was having a seizure.

The heart disease that had been plaguing David Hennigan, as I had been told several years earlier, had taken his life.

With his passing went the still unanswered questions held so long by the family of Irene Izak.

EPILOGUE

I stood at a bedside in a nursing home, conducting the most difficult of interviews. I was speaking with Dave Fleming on the evening of June 5, 2001, challenging the memory of a former New York state trooper who had been "laid up" for nearly twenty-four years. Understanding him was a challenge.

Fleming, with the state police since June 1962, had been the first trooper, other than David Hennigan, to arrive at the scene of Irene Izak's murder. He was therefore the first cop to observe Hennigan's demeanor. I believed, as I'm sure Ray Polett and Charlie Donoghue believed thirty-three years earlier, on June 10, 1968, that Fleming's observations could be revealing.

I had come to know Fleming early in the 1970s in my role as a young police reporter. I had found him to be likeable, easy to get along with and cooperative. I was saddened when the career of one of the "good guys" came to a tragic and abrupt end.

He was off duty early on the morning of July 31, 1977, when he drove his pickup truck off the side of a state road in Jefferson County. The truck overturned in a ditch, and he was ejected. When he emerged from a coma about a month later in a Syracuse, New York hospital, he was partially paralyzed. At forty-two, he retired from state police in June 1978.

Having not seen Fleming in the subsequent two decades, I was admittedly embarrassed to now be seeking him out to ask about the events he had observed on Wellesley Island. One of his retired colleagues interceded for me, obtaining Fleming's consent for an interview.

At times he was confused, and occasionally I had to ask him to repeat his muffled and strained phrases, which were frequently interrupted by coughing spells. But his recollections of that fateful morning in 1968 seemed firm, and he was resolute in his opinions.

As I bid him goodbye that evening, I promised to make a return visit. I failed in that commitment, and six months later, on December 6, he died. He was sixty-seven.

Tragedy also awaited another state trooper who played a small role in the Izak case. Sergeant Gerald DeGroot, who as desk officer at the Watertown headquarters took Trooper Hennigan's radio calls about the vehicle stop on Interstate 81 and, later, about the homicide, was killed in a head-on collision on June 24, 1978, in Watertown. The twenty-one-year state police veteran had just gone off duty and was on his way home. Watertown police said the other driver was intoxicated and crossed into the sergeant's lane of travel. DeGroot, forty-eight, had dedicated a share of his career to the prevention of drinking and driving and to the rehabilitation of convicted drunk drivers.

Trooper James McCarthy, who according to former investigator Charles Donoghue saw on Trooper Hennigan's unmarked police car a spot that appeared to be blood, died at age fifty-seven in 1987 following a lengthy illness.

Having Donoghue assist me in my review of the Izak case was somewhat of a surprise because he and I did not hit it off so well in our earlier years. My one memory of working with him is my attempt to report an arrest he had made and his reaction being a threat to arrest me for interfering in that particular investigation.

When he wanted the *Watertown Daily Times* to dust off the cobwebs in the Wellesley Island murder mystery, he expressed his viewpoints to one of my colleagues, Larry Cole. Only after Cole had died, and after the private detective, Gus Papay, had visited with him, did Donoghue put past differences behind and work with me.

Donoghue, having retired as a state police senior investigator in August 1974, was suffering from cancer at the time of our joint effort. He was seventy-two when he died on August 10, 2004.

Ray Polett was with the New York State Police for twenty years. He retired to accept appointment by New York governor Hugh L. Carey in June 1978 to fill an unfinished term as Lewis County sheriff in Lowville, New York. He failed to win election to his own term and in 1980 was hired as police chief for the Upper Dublin Township, near Philadelphia. He retired ten years later to Lake Wynonah, Pennsylvania, and has since settled in Punta Gorda, Florida.

Like Polett, Bill McClusky left one job to accept a governor's appointment to another. In 1973, Governor Nelson Rockefeller placed him on the Jefferson County Court bench. And like Polett, he was unable to win the public vote for his own term. He was still active in a private law practice when, at sixty-eight, on October 3, 2004, he suffered a fatal head injury in an accidental fall down some stairs in his home.

Peter J. Burns, the fourth trooper (behind Hennigan, Fleming and Amyot) on the Wellesley Island scene, rose in the ranks to become a captain. As a lieutenant, he was commander of the Watertown zone from 1986 to 1994. He is now retired.

So, too, are Thomas P. Connelly and Stanley Weidman. Connelly was promoted to captain in February 1999 and was placed in command of the Watertown zone. In that position, he was no longer involved in the Izak investigation. Weidman, the chief investigator in the revived Izak probe, retired soon after the case stalled into its latest lull. He declined my request for an interview.

Senior Investigator Ladue remained on duty at Watertown and was the primary officer in following up any leads in the 1968 murder. But any of my inquiries to him about the case were referred to higher-ranking officers in Oneida, who maintained a "no comment" position. Illness forced Ladue to retire at age fifty-eight in April 2007.

Ladue, while working on his boat at a dock at Clayton, New York, fell into the St. Lawrence River on August 25, 2010. His body was recovered by a dive team early the next morning. He was alone at the time. State police believed his health may have caused his fall.

Clifford F. Putman, the toll collector who was the last person to see Irene Izak alive, other than her killer, continued to work for the Thousand Islands Bridge Authority into 1973. He was eighty-one when he died in September 1986. He left no survivors. His funeral was at Our Lady of the Sacred Heart Catholic Church in Watertown.

As for Irene's Volkswagen, Papay tried to track it down, hoping against hope that it still existed for forensic tests that were not available in 1968. He determined that Mario Galetto of Old Forge, Pennsylvania, just south of Scranton, was the last registered owner. Galetto had purchased the car from a used car dealer in Old Forge. The VW "wasn't a fast car," he told Papay. Galetto eventually traded it, and no other trace of the car can be found.

APPENDIX A

FAMILY LETTER TO NEW YORK GOVERNOR GEORGE E. PATAKI

Waterford Road
Box 395-RD#3
Dalton, PA 18414
Tel: [deleted]

September 18, 1998

Honorable George E. Pataki
Governor
State of New York
State Capital
Albany, NY 12224

Re: Requesting your help concerning the investigation of the unsolved murder of Miss Irene J. Izak, which occurred on June 10, 1968 in Watertown, NY (Jefferson County).

Dear Governor Pataki:

It is the deep pain and everlasting sorrow which compels us to write you and ask for your help in our plight to seek justice for our beloved sister Irene Izak who was brutally beaten and murdered 30 years ago, on June 10, 1968, while she was heading to Canada and traveling alone on I-81 through upper New York State.

The perpetrator(s) of this heinous crime has never been identified or apprehended and the case remains open with investigators from Troop "D" of the New York State Police.

Our parents, Rev. Bohdan and Maria Izak, grieved constantly over Irene's death and did not live long enough to find out why her young life was cut short. It is so unfair that they were unable to see the day when justice would prevail. Father died in December 1988 and mother passed away in November 1991.

Our family, which included five of us children, lived in Ukraine until 1944. We were persecuted by both the Nazis and the Soviet Communists and had to escape tyranny. It took us four years as displaced persons to finally reach the United States. As a 10-year-old girl, I clearly remember the day we arrived in America and saw the Statue of Liberty. Our father told us: "We will be free now, we won't have to worry about anybody hurting us ever again." Little did he know that a horrible hurt awaited us some day in our new home. Just as your grandparents must have been emotionally overwhelmed and proud when they arrived in this wonderful land. Even though we came from a totalitarian country, our parents taught us to always respect authority and the laws of our adoptive country.

In June 1968 our father had the nightmarish task of traveling from Scranton PA to Watertown NY to identify and bring home the bludgeoned body of our beloved sister Irene.

There were two significant statements that our father made to our family which we will never forget as long as we live. He said that when he began crying at the morgue upon seeing Irene's body, all the State Troopers expressed their condolences to him except the Trooper who claimed to have found Irene's body. This was the same Trooper who stopped my sister 30 minutes earlier on I-81 for allegedly speeding and had my sister's blood stains and splatter on his uniform from the scene of the incident. Our father also sadly remarked to us: "It looks like they are covering for one of their own." He made this same statement a number of times until the day he died.

We have tried to cope with the untimely loss of our sister and we have placed our confidence in the hands of the State Police Investigators, who were struggling to solve the case and bring her murderer to justice. As 30 long years went by, day after day we anxiously waited for that telephone call which would have told us that Irene's murderer was arrested and charged, but that call never came. Investigator Raymond O. Polett of the BCI was originally assigned to the case but he retired in May 1978. Subsequently Investigator Robert S. Cooke took over the case, but unfortunately no significant progress was made in the case and he retired in May 1998. Presently, we understand that Senior Investigator Robert [*sic*] L. Ladue has the case, but he has never contacted us and to the best of our knowledge the case is only updated on a 6-month time period, but no active investigative work is being conducted on it.

Further, in a published article appearing in the *Watertown Daily Times* of June 11, 1998, Lieutenant Thomas Connelly was interviewed about the case and stated to a reporter: "There are some things I like to see done, I will discuss this with our investigators. I may want to have some interviews done again. Of course the chances of solving this decreases as time goes by, but it will remain an open case until all possible suspects would have to be dead." His statement was not very reassuring or encouraging to us and we did not see any subsequent good faith efforts being made by the investigators. In fact it took several letters written by our daughter Lisa Ewasko Caputo before Lt. Connelly even acknowledged that we existed. Finally, he mailed us Irene's wrist watch and her gold high school graduation ring. To this date, we know of no recent investigative effort that has been made by the State Police in order to solve this case.

Our daughter, Lisa, has been somewhat obsessed with the unsolved murder of her Aunt Irene, and she has been the "family spokesperson" when letters had to be written and when phone calls had to be made. In her relentless efforts to seek out the truth, she sought help from Private Investigators on the Internet. In June of this year she located Detective Augustine Papay Jr., who is a retired New York City Detective and a licensed Private Investigator in New York State. Detective Papay, who has a very extensive investigative background in Police Department Internal Affairs and in the Homicide investigative fields, has agreed to take this case at no charge to us.

On July 4, 1998, we officially retained Detective Papay as our "private investigator" and have granted him full Power of Attorney to obtain records, consult with law enforcement officials, review evidence and to fully investigate this matter. Since he began his probe of the case, Detective Papay has interviewed numerous retired State Police personnel, all of whom unanimously expressed their opinions and theories about this case. In addition, based on interviews which Detective Papay conducted with retired State Troopers, investigators, newspapers columnists and people who knew the subject, the following alarming facts were uncovered about retired State Trooper David N. Hennigan:

He stopped Irene for allegedly speeding on I-81 and alleged that she was going 75/mph, however according to Investigator Polett when he tested the vehicle it would barely reach 65/mph, raising suspicion that Irene's car stop was not based on legitimate law enforcement reasons.

Who according to our late father, did not offer his condolences to him at the morgue when he went to claim Irene's body.

Who according to former BCI investigators, gave approximately three different versions of events to fellow Troopers as to how he got Irene's blood on his uniform.

Based on interviews conducted by Detective Papay, witnesses have related that the subject has a history of domestic violence and violent rage attacks.

Who has a history of being involved with pornographic materials while on duty, as related by his coworkers.

Whose official statement and alibi was never satisfactory and was clearly questionable by supervisors and BCI investigators.

Whose official police raincoat which he was wearing on the night of the murder may be missing to this day.

Based on an interview conducted by State Police of the Toll Collector at the Thousand Island Bridge, it was revealed that Irene expressed an emotion of fear of Trooper Hennigan and she questioned the toll collector about police procedures concerning the stopping of motorists.

Who routinely requested the Desk Sergeant to give him an unmarked police vehicle to patrol his post.

Who was called "The Heathen" by fellow Troopers, yet became an ordained deacon in the Roman Church after the murder of Irene.

This is the same individual who has always been considered a prime suspect in her murder.

Governor, we are not writing this letter to you to wrongfully accuse a former member of the New York State Police of murdering our sister. We are also not accusing any member of the Division of New York State Police of a "cover-up" in the criminal investigation which has remained open for over 30 years. We have trusted the State Police all this time and we were content that as professional law enforcement officers they would deal with this case as professionals should. However, with all due respect to their service, their profession and their dedication, we as reasonable common folks cannot willfully ignore the ten (10) elements of facts noted above, and therefore we have serious questions to raise with the New York State Police. These ten (10) elements were uncovered and verified by our private investigator in the very short amount of time that he has investigated this case.

We know that the Division of New York State Police is a semi military style police force whose ranking commanders are very concerned about the image of the members of their Department. We sincerely hope that the Troop "D" Division Commanders from 1968 to 1998 were not trying to protect their untouchable image of their members, whereby they also may have blindly and unwillingly protected the murderer of our sister.

We also know that since 1968 new forensic technology has become available to law enforcement investigators in the field of forensic science. Latent fingerprints, which were unidentifiable in 1968, can now be positively identified by a computer called SAFIS.

Identification of stains of blood-chemical and microscopic analyses are necessary to identify blood and DNA. Analysis of blood evidence which is now available to investigators is necessary to positively include or exclude a person as a perpetrator of the crime. The victim's clothing must be examined for possible seminal and saliva stain grouping tests. Witnesses, especially retired State Police personnel, who may have been reluctant to come forward with information in 1968 should be re-interviewed to obtain oral testimony and to build a psychological profile of the suspect. The retired Trooper's personnel file should be reviewed for prior history of disciplinary cases including allegations of "unwanted sexual advances towards women" and use of excessive or unnecessary force against civilians. Investigators must look for any written requisition for a new raincoat by the suspected Trooper. The most important physical evidence is considered to be the blood stained and blood splattered uniform which the Trooper was wearing on the night of the murder. This important piece of physical evidence should be examined by a "blood splatter expert" who will be able to conclusively determine if the person who was wearing this uniform is the same person who may have committed this crime. We believe that the FBI national criminal laboratory has such experts available and would be able to assist the New York State Police if the State Police forensic laboratory lacks such expertise. And finally, investigators from BCI must confer with and work closely with the office of the Honorable Jim King who is the Jefferson County District Attorney so that a Grand Jury may be impaneled to examine all the evidence.

In conclusion, there are three basic things we would hope to accomplish by writing you this letter and are making the following requests:

Please have your office appoint a liaison person who would assist our private investigator, Detective Papay, in the submission of any newly discovered evidence to the New York State Police, and who would ensure that any new leads uncovered by the State Police or by our Private Investigator are followed up by the assigned BCI investigator and are submitted to the office of the District Attorney as soon as possible. The liaison would also ensure that our Private Investigator would be able to examine some of the physical and documentary evidence as an "in camera" examination, and that he would have access to certain agency records under Article 6 of the Freedom of Information Law.

That the Superintendent of State Police resubmit all physical evidence to the State Police Forensic Laboratory for Serology, DNA, and Latent Print examinations utilizing the latest equipment available in forensic technology.

That the Superintendent of State Police submit the blood stained/splattered uniform held in evidence at Oneida to the FBI national crime laboratory for a detailed examination by a "blood splatter expert."

Governor Pataki, we will deeply appreciate any help and cooperation which your office can provide us under these sad and unfortunate circumstances. While we are not New York State residents, we are hopeful that our plight to seek justice for our sister Irene will not be in vain.

We will remain eternally grateful to you for your help and look forward to hearing from you.

Sincerely,
Helen Izak Ewasko
Paul S. Ewasko

APPENDIX B
LETTERS TO DAVID HENNIGAN

123 S. Main St.
Taylor, PA 18517

November 2000

Rev. David Hennigan
Deacon Assistant
Church of Our Lady of the Sacred Heart
664 Thompson St.
Watertown, NY 13601

Dear Deacon Hennigan,

My name is Lisa Caputo. I am the niece of Irene Izak. I am hoping and praying that you will be kind enough to read this letter in full and then will find it in your heart to respond.

As you know there has been a renewed investigation into my aunt's murder. The NY State Police are not telling us everything. I have been told that you may have had something to do with her murder, but I don't know what to believe or want to believe that. Over the past 32 years our family has been kept in the dark. We have learned things from the news media, whether fact or fiction.

I'm hoping that you will tell my family what your recollection of that night was. There have been many times over the past many years that I have wanted to pick up the phone and call you or write, but I didn't want to intrude on your life. I am now 37 years old, and have been haunted by my aunt's murder since I was 4 years old. I've now come to the point where I feel I must write to you and pray that you will be compassionate enough to respond to my plea.

While I was just a child when my aunt was taken away from us, I still have special memories of her, however, there is one memory that will be with me till the day I die. I can still remember the day my father unexpectedly came from work in the middle of the afternoon. My mother was making my siblings and me ice cream cones when he walked in and asked us to please go outside. I will never forget hearing my mother's screams and sobs when he told her that her sister was murdered. That was the day that changed my entire family's lives forever.

We have had to imagine the fright and terror my aunt must have gone through that night. It is a horrible thing to have to live with. Try to imagine this and then think if it was your wife, daughter, mother, aunt, niece or granddaughter. Then I think you can imagine what we have gone through and hopefully you will find it in your heart to tell us what your recollections of that night was. We have read or heard secondhand events that occurred that night. We are trying to learn the truth and to find some peace and healing. Whoever took her from us has apparently gone on to enjoy life, while my family has had to endure the pain and deal with not knowing why Irene was taken from us.

My Aunt Irene was a kind and loving person. She had hopes and dreams. She graduated from our local university and then traveled to Paris to study at the Sorbonne, and then became a teacher. She was the fifth of six children in her family and was born in Ukraine. My grandfather was a Byzantine Rite Catholic priest. He and my grandmother were witnesses to persecutions by Nazis and Soviet Communists when they lived in Ukraine, so they brought their family to the United States believing they would be safe and free here, however their dream was shattered on June 10, 1968. My grandparents suffered unimaginable grief and a part of them died when she died. We too continue to grieve for Irene and want to try to understand why someone took her from us.

Could it have been a random act of violence? Maybe this person didn't originally intend to murder her? I keep thinking about the Commandment "Thou shalt not kill," and that maybe her killer accidentally killed her. I so want to believe the latter since we have been told that she was not robbed or sexually assaulted.

Over the years I keep praying that my aunt's murderer will make peace with God, our family, his family and himself and come forward to tell what happened that night. Our faith helps us a great deal, and we know that my aunt is with the Lord. At the same time we believe that the person who took her life will be accountable to the same God for what he has done.

While I know you may not have all the answers that my family seeks, I'm hoping that you will find it in your heart to fill in some of the blanks and reach out to us as you were one of the last persons to see her alive.

I am now married and have two small children of my own. The only way my children will ever know Aunt Irene is though my family's memories and our visits to the cemetery. Until my Heavenly Father decides to take me home, I will always grieve for my aunt and search for the truth.

Thank you very much for taking the time to read this letter. Once again, I ask for your help and hope that you will respond to this letter. I don't know what else to say except that I hope you will help us.

Sincerely,
Lisa Ewasko Caputo

The letter went unanswered.

David C. Shampine
23292 Gardner Drive
Watertown, NY 13601

Jan. 26, 2001

Mr. & Mrs. David N. Hennigan
20971 County Route 59
Dexter, NY 13631

Dear Mr. & Mrs. Hennigan:

As you might have suspected, I have been anticipating writing a book about the life and death of Irene Izak. But what has come as a surprise to me is the recent expression of interest by a Los Angeles screenwriter to do a movie script about the Izak case.

Late in November, I met in Los Angeles with the writer, Mr. Ed Nast, and with his agent, Mr. Jack Scagnetti, as discussions continued toward that end. Prior to that, Mr. Nast visited me at the *Watertown Daily Times* building, at which time he made known his interest.

While I assume that you hold a degree of contempt against me, I want to assure you of my hopes of fairly representing you in the book. I would like to present your life stories, and to give you every opportunity to present your account, your side of the story, of what occurred on the night of June 9–10, 1968, and of the days and years that followed.

My goal is to compile a balanced presentation, and I submit that it would be in your best interests to interview with me for that purpose. I ask that you contact me at your earliest convenience.

Respectfully,
David C. Shampine

My letter was answered by an attorney.

David C. Shampine
23292 Gardner Drive
Watertown, NY 13601

Aug. 6, 2004

David N. Hennigan
c/o Our Lady of The Sacred Heart Church
664 Thompson St.
Watertown, NY 13601

Dear Dave:

As I'm sure you recall, I wrote you in January 2001 requesting an interview for the purpose of presenting your story in a book about the death of Irene Izak. You declined through an attorney.

It has taken longer than expected, but I have completed six of my intended seven chapters. Again, I want to be fair to you, and ask that you reconsider. Even if you would prefer not to discuss the events of June 9–10, 1968, I would still like to chat with you about your career as a trooper, your volunteer work and your choice of service as a deacon in the Catholic Church.

If you consent, and if you so choose, you could take this opportunity to set the record straight that you are not the same person as described by some of your former colleagues in the New York State Police.

As before, I ask that you contact me at your earliest convenience.

Respectfully,
Dave Shampine

In a letter dated August 12, 2004, Hennigan declined my request. I responded with a letter urging him to have a private meeting with representatives of the Izak family to answer their questions, promising I would not report those discussions, if he so wished. He did not respond, nor did the family hear from him.

ABOUT THE AUTHOR

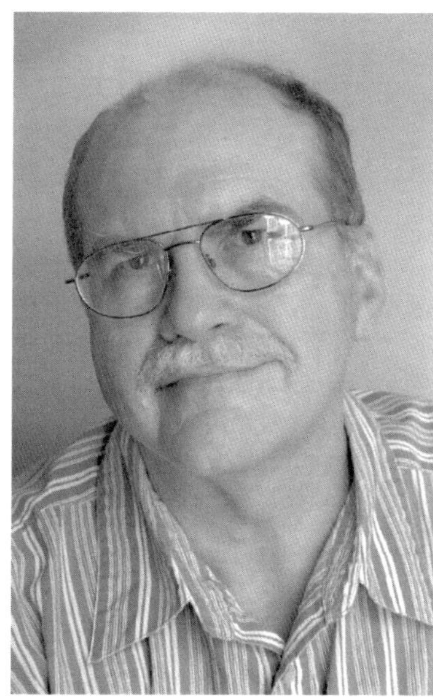

Dave Shampine, a lifelong resident of Jefferson County, New York, has been a reporter for the *Watertown Daily Times* since 1971, with the majority of his career focused on crime reporting. He has written his history column, "Times Gone By," for the past twelve years and is also a contributing writer and copyeditor for the *Bulletin* of the Jefferson County Historical Society in Watertown. He is the author of *Remembering New York's North County: Tales from Times Gone By* and *Colorful Characters of Northern New York: Northern Lights*, both published by The History Press.

He has received awards from the New York State Bar Association, New York Newspaper Publishers Association, New York State Associated Press Association and the Jefferson Community College Alumni Association, which honored him with a professional achievement award.